Beehives, Barbecues, Fireplaces and More

How to Build an Inviting Outdoor Entertainment Area

15 Spectacular Plans • Complete Material Lists • Basic Instructions

D1449892

by Kathy James

Published by Beehive Publications, Scottsdale, AZ

Beehives, Barbecues, Fireplaces and More:
How to Build an Inviting Outdoor Entertainment Area

KEJ 14229 LLC
2630 North Granite Reef Road
Scottsdale, Arizona 85257

Fax all orders to:
(267) 880-1474 or (480) 949-0746

The plans, elevations, and three-dimensional architectural illustrations contained in this book were prepared by a licensed architect in the state of Arizona. They are presented as dimensioned drawings to convey the intent of the designs as received by the architect from the author and designer. The owner/builder shall be responsible for verifying all dimensions, block sizing, material quantities, and structural requirements to comply with all pertinent local and national building codes prior to construction. The owner shall also be responsible for all code and structural requirements when deviating from these plans. The author and the publisher cannot assume or accept any responsibility or liability, including liability for negligence, for errors or oversights in this data and information and in the use of such information.

Library of Congress Cataloging-in-Publication Data

James, Kathy, 1953–
Beehives, barbecues, fireplaces, and more : how to build an inviting outdoor entertainment area : 15 spectacular plans, complete materials lists, basic instructions by Kathy James. - - 1st ed. 2nd ed. 3rd ed. 4th ed.
p. cm.
Includes index.
ISBN 0-9706742-0-1
1. Barbecues (Fireplaces)- -Design and construction- -Amateurs' manuals. I. Title.

TH4961.5 .J36 2001
643.55- -dc21

00-052084
Published by: Beehive Publications

Printed by: Tri Star Visual Communications, Phoenix, Arizona

Publishing Consultant

Linda F. Radke, Five Star Publications, Inc.

Editorial Consultant

Paul M. Howey

Cover Design

Jeff Yesh

Interior Design and Typesetting

Kim Scott

Illustrator

Jeff Yesh

Landscape Illustrator

Darrel Biggs

Photographers

Herb Stokes and Mark Boisclair

Proofreaders

Frankie Joe Harrell and Carla Harrell McClanahan

Indexer

Joy Dean Lee

Dedication

To my daughters Nicole and Kristen
You have been my sounding board throughout the writing of this book, follow your dreams.

To my brother Frank and his wife Diane:
Thanks for always encouraging me to stick with it…you were right—it came together.

And thank you to all of the individuals who gave endless hours to this project!

About the Author

A member of the American Society of Interior Designers, Kathy James is the owner of Sonoran Oasis Images, a residential landscape and design firm located in Scottsdale, Arizona. "We design and build it all," she explains, "from hardscaping to landscaping." She defines "hardscaping" as exterior structures including beehive fireplaces, barbecue grills, banco (bench) seating, custom masonry installations, and water features such as waterfalls, ponds, spas, and swimming pools.

Kathy creates designs that blend into their natural surroundings and adapt to any architectural style. She works with builders and landscapers from areas as diverse as Pennsylvania, New Mexico, and Arizona. Among her clientele are such entertainment notables as Gene Hackman and Val Kilmer. She is a romantic by nature and free-spirited by choice, and these two traits are the starting point for all her designs.

Perhaps one of her most elaborate creations is her own home, which she built to be a showcase of the types of work her company offers. The elements of earth, fire, and water are represented both inside and outside the house. Among the home's four water features are an indoor boulder water wall, an outdoor spa, and 35' lap pool which has underneath the waterfall a firepit tucked away in the corner to make it look as though the water is on fire. She also built a cobblestone fireplace in the living room, a beehive fireplace on the patio (with a grill and television), and talks of adding a corner fire pit in the master bedroom! An advocate of outdoor entertaining, her entire dining room is built on the patio, with heaters for cool winter evenings and misters for the summer.

Kathy really enjoys working on special design features with homeowners and builders, and is definitely looking at this book as the start of future design books for the outdoors.

Table of Contents

Introduction

Ever wish your home were larger? Perhaps you've thought about building an addition, but were discouraged by the cost? There is a less expensive alternative. You can expand your living space economically and beautifully by creating an outdoor entertainment area in your own backyard.

All the plans in this book encompass one thing in common: the element of fire—fire to create a relaxing and even romantic mood, fire to push back the edges of darkness, fire for warmth, and fire with which to cook. These designs range from the simplest of concepts to the more elaborate; from the fire pit of our primitive ancestors to a combination fireplace, barbecue, bench, and bar (complete with refrigerator and sink!).

These plans were created and developed over the years exclusively for our clients, and this is the first time they've ever been offered in a book. In these pages, you will find a style to fit nearly every architectural need, from modern to Southwestern to Mediterranean; and every geographic location from the Catskill Mountains of New York to the Sonoran Desert of Arizona. When you're finished, you'll have a special place to relax by yourself on a quiet evening or to host a party for all of your friends.

Whether you plan to build your own outdoor entertainment area or hire someone to do it for you, this book contains everything you need to know. I've included basic masonry techniques, construction plans for these 15 designs (including the extremely popular beehive fireplace), and a complete materials list for each project.

Wondering how to get started? I'd suggest looking through the landscape illustrations and photographs that I've included in this book, and then take a stroll around your own yard. Before you know it, you'll soon be seeing your outdoor areas in new and creative ways! I think you'll be excited at the possibilities. Soon you'll be hearing the crackling of the fire, entranced by its flickering light, and savoring the flavor of food grilled over an open flame.

Working with Your Chosen Design

If you took that walk suggested in the Intro-duction, your head is probably swimming with all the possibilities. Once you've made your final design selection, here are some other things to consider before getting started:

Site the Plan

If your goal is to use your outdoor entertainment area to create a visual extension of your indoor living space, start inside the house. Look out the windows to where you envision building your outdoor fireplace or barbecue. Then, if possible, try to position the addition where it will add to your visual enjoyment from inside the house, as well as when you're outside.

Check Next Door

If your proposed construction will be on the property line or in some other way visible from your neighbor's lot, it would probably be a good idea to discuss your plans with them and get their approval. (Most likely, all they'll want in return is an invitation when you're all finished!) And if you're not sure of the precise location of your property lines, you'd be well advised to have them surveyed before you start. Even that nice neighbor who approved your project in exchange for a barbecued steak dinner might have to move, and you can never be certain that the person who buys his house is going to be quite as accommodating.

Plan Ahead for the Utilities

If you're going to need electricity and/or natural gas for your addition, you'll want to locate the addition in an ideal spot to minimize the expense of installing these utilities without sacrificing any visual benefits. Consult an electrician and/or natural gas (propane/LP) expert before you start construction. This could save you a lot of money and a headache. You'll want to meet with your licensed contractors prior to pouring the founda-tion so that you can install the utilities according to your local governing code.

Site the plan.

Maximize Privacy

You don't want people looking in your living room windows, and you probably won't want to position your outdoor entertainment area in full display to the neighborhood either. To the greatest extent possible, utilize existing privacy screening (*e.g.*, walls, fences, trees, or other barriers) when finding the ideal spot for your addition, but make certain you allow for adequate clearance for obvious fire safety reasons. (Your local building codes will have a lot to say about exactly where you can build outdoor fireplaces and barbecues.)

Plan for Seating

For maximum enjoyment, be sure to include places to sit and enjoy the new addition to your backyard. Of course, patio chairs and chaise lounges will work great, but you might want to consider one of the modified plans contained in this book that features the inclusion of bench seating to the original design. (These benches are also a great place to show off your potted plants and flowers!)

Plan for seating.

Building Codes

Your initial reaction might be, "I'm adding this fireplace or barbecue to my own property myself, I don't need to get involved with city hall." Wrong. Granted, the array of building codes and specifications might seem arbitrary at first, but they exist for a purpose. Building codes help ensure quality construction for your particular geographical location. Codes vary widely from one part of the country to the other, due primarily to the diversity of climates (and particularly the differences in depth that ground freezes and thaws in a large part of the U.S.).

Be sure to comply with the building codes in your area (including any regulations regarding how far back from your property line you must build); otherwise, it could prove costly. For example, if your house is inspected, you might be required to tear out the construction and rebuild it. Also, it may be impossible to sell your house if building codes are ignored.

Stop by your local building department to get any required building permits.

As soon as you're ready—but *before* you've begun construction—stop by your local building department and get any required building permits. Here's what you should take with you (but you might want to call first to determine if there's anything else they require):

Detailed Site Plans

Prepare a scale drawing of your property (you can trace it from your blueprints or draw it yourself from your own measurements) and show the precise location of your proposed addition fireplace or barbecue.

Construction Plans

Take photocopies of the pertinent building plans from this book to show the proposed method of construction.

Materials List

Provide a complete list of all the materials that will be used in the construction (included with the designs in this book). Local regulations may require using slightly different materials, and you'll want to know before you order them.

If a building permit is required, you'll be informed as to the stages of construction at which inspection and approval must take place. (Note: Never attempt to proceed beyond these checkpoints without having your work inspected.) By being prepared, thorough and careful in your construction techniques, your inspector is likely to be quite impressed.

Safety First!

If you don't keep yourself and others safe during the construction phase, it's going to be a little difficult to enjoy your outdoor entertainment area when it's finished! The greatest safety aid ever utilized is *common sense.* Use it and stay safe. The following is a limited list of safety considerations to keep in mind:

Lift with Your Legs

The materials used in masonry construction are heavy. Don't bend over to pick up a sack of mortar or even a concrete block. Bend your knees and lift with your legs!

Buddy System

Constructing these additions is physical, manual labor. If you're not used to it, get some friends to help. Work just a few hours each day and take frequent rest breaks. And drink plenty of water, especially if you're working in a warm climate.

Gloves and Safety Glasses

You should wear these at all times during the construction of your project, but especially when you're sawing or cutting concrete block, brick, or stone, and when you're mixing and pouring concrete (it's also a good idea to wear a disposable face mask). When using power tools, be sure to wear **ear protectors** as well.

safety glasses

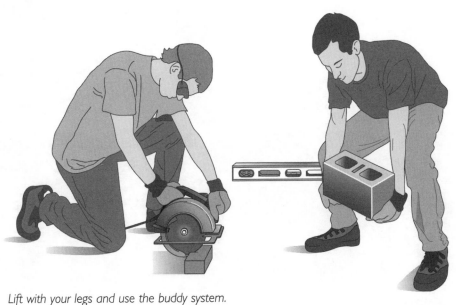

Lift with your legs and use the buddy system.

Call Before You Dig

Contact your local utility companies (*i.e.*, electric, water, natural gas, telephone, cable, or other service provider) before you begin your project. They are required to come to your house at no charge and mark the locations of any buried utility lines. *Do not begin digging until they tell you exactly where the lines are located.*

Power Tools

Be sure to follow the safety instructions that came with the tools. If you need to use an extension cord, make certain that it's of the proper gauge to handle the amperage of the tool. Only plug tools into a GFCI (Ground Fault Circuit Interrupter) outlet. Don't use any power tool when either the ground or the tool is wet. Don't use power tools when the cords are frayed. Use only sharp bits and blades in your drill and saw. And don't push your power tools beyond their capabilities or use them for purposes for which they were not intended.

Other Masonry Projects

This book contains the key things you need to know in order to construct the fireplaces, barbecues, and benches shown in these pages. If you're also planning to build a patio, sidewalk, stairs, or other masonry construction project, you'll need to consult the building codes in your area and other books on those subjects (the materials and techniques used vary quite a bit from what are needed to build the designs in this book).

Contact your local utility companies before you begin your project.

Tools

As with any task, always use the right tool for the right job. If you use a tool for a purpose other than that for which it was intended, you're asking for trouble! With masonry work, the tools are fairly basic and they're relatively inexpensive. So, whenever possible, buy a better grade of tool (especially if it's one you're likely to use on more than one project) and you'll be happier in the long run.

Tools Needed for Building Concrete Footers

Concrete block and other masonry walls need to be built on a base of concrete (called a *footer*) that extends beneath the frost or freeze line (your local building codes will contain specific information for your area) in order to keep the wall from cracking as the ground freezes and thaws. Here's what you'll need in the way of tools and why they are important:

Pointed Spade for digging the hole for the footer

Square Shovel for cleaning up the straight lines of the hole

Mortar Hoe (also known as a ***Mason's Hoe***), which resembles a regular garden hoe except that it has two large holes in the blade to aid in the mixing of concrete and other masonry materials

Wheelbarrow for hauling materials and mixing concrete (it should be a heavy-duty wheelbarrow capable of holding approximately three cubic feet of material and have pneumatic tires)

Powered Concrete Mixer, with either an electric motor or a gasoline engine, can save you a lot of effort and time on larger jobs (these are available from tool rental agencies)

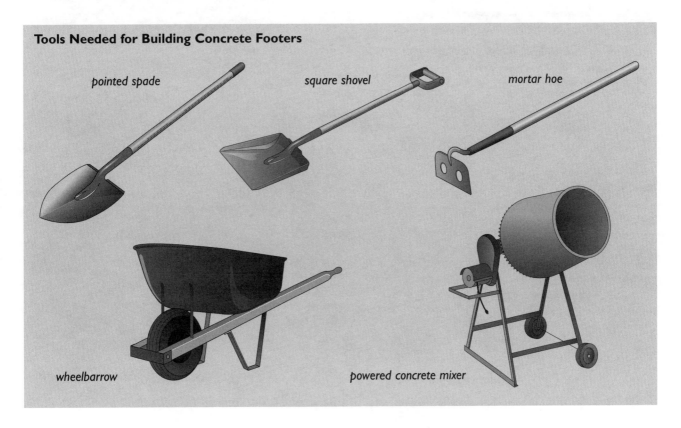

Tools Needed for Building Concrete Footers

pointed spade · square shovel · mortar hoe

wheelbarrow · powered concrete mixer

Tools Needed for Measuring and Leveling

Take precise measurements before beginning your project, and then take them again! There is no substitute for accuracy in construction, especially when working with something as permanent as concrete. You probably already have a lot of these items in your toolbox. If not, this is a perfect excuse to make a trip to the hardware or home building supply store and add to your collection (tell your spouse I said you need to have these)! Here's what you should have:

Carpenter's Level, at least three feet long (preferably four feet)

Torpedo Level, to level in tight corners

Folding Rule, which is similar to a tape measure, but literally folds to fit in your pocket

Tape Measure, at least 25 feet long (preferably 50 feet)

Carpenter's Square (also known as a **Framing Square**), to check the squareness of joints and corners

Grease Pencil, to mark your materials

Chalk Line, Mason's Cord, and **Line Level**, for laying out the wall and making certain it's both vertical and level during the construction process

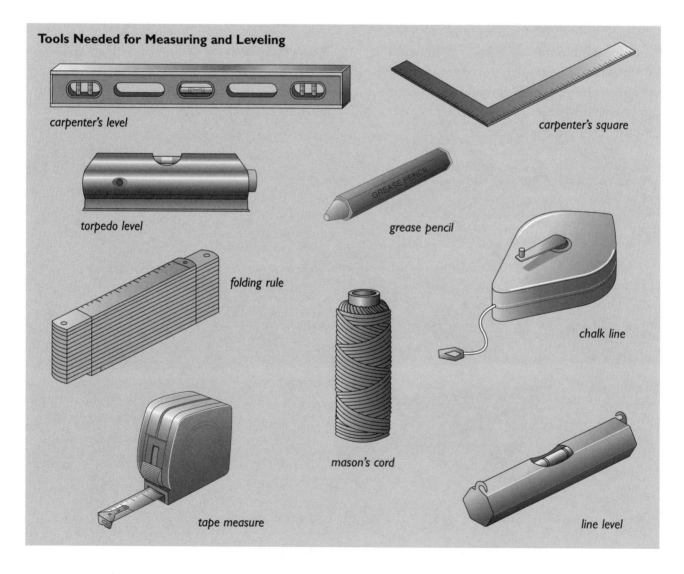

Tools Needed for Measuring and Leveling

carpenter's level

carpenter's square

torpedo level

grease pencil

folding rule

chalk line

mason's cord

tape measure

line level

Tools Needed for Cutting Block, Brick, and Stone

The ideal job would be one in which there was no need for cutting any of the building materials. (If you have such an ideal job, call me…I'd love to work on it!) Cutting masonry building materials sounds tough, but you'll quickly get the hang of it, especially if you're using the right tools (be sure and wear protective goggles and gloves):

Circular Saw with a Masonry Blade can be used for cutting concrete block (with a wood cutting blade, you'll also use the saw to cut the boards for the form for the footer)

Grinder (with 4" or 4½" diamond drill blade) for cutting flagstone

Wet Saw for cutting tile and certain types of stone/slate

Brick Set Chisel (also known as a ***Mason's Chisel***) and ***Bricklayer's Hammer*** will help you to split and shape bricks and stone to fit your design

Tools Needed for Cutting Block, Brick, and Stone

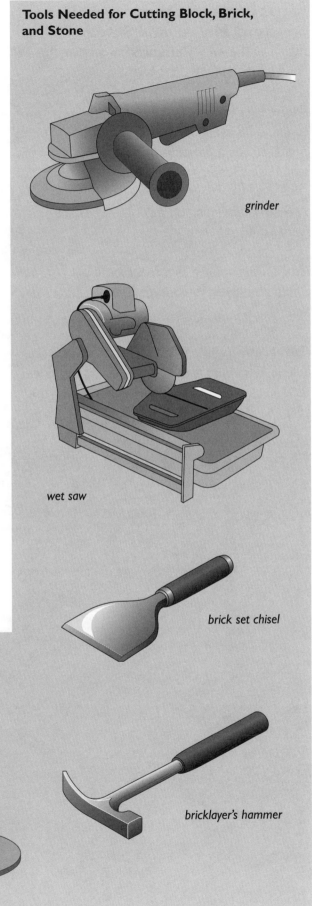

grinder

wet saw

brick set chisel

bricklayer's hammer

circular saw

Tools Needed for Working with Concrete, Mortar, and Stucco

These are the tools you'll need to prepare the soil and to finish off the concrete and mortar:

Tamper for compacting the soil prior to pouring concrete. It's available either as a hand tool or, for larger jobs, as a power tool (both are available at rental agencies)

Screed for finishing off a concrete surface before it dries

Hawk (also known as a ***Hock***), a small board with a handle on the bottom for carrying mortar and stucco

Grout Stop (made of plastic or paper and available in 100' rolls) is used to put on top of block cells so concrete doesn't fall down through the cells (used as a mortar barrier)

Trowel for applying mortar

Mortar Jointer (also known as a ***Sled Jointer***) for compacting and shaping the mortar between the blocks, bricks, or stones in your wall

Brush for cleaning excess mortar from your wall while the mortar is still wet

Plasterer's Rake for scratching the first coat of stucco (you can also make your own by driving a row of nails (placed one inch apart) through an 18" long 2×2 board)

Cement Backer Board, a glass cement mesh used for interior/exterior that looks like silver drywall and gets attached to the stone/wood surface as preparation for a stone veneer

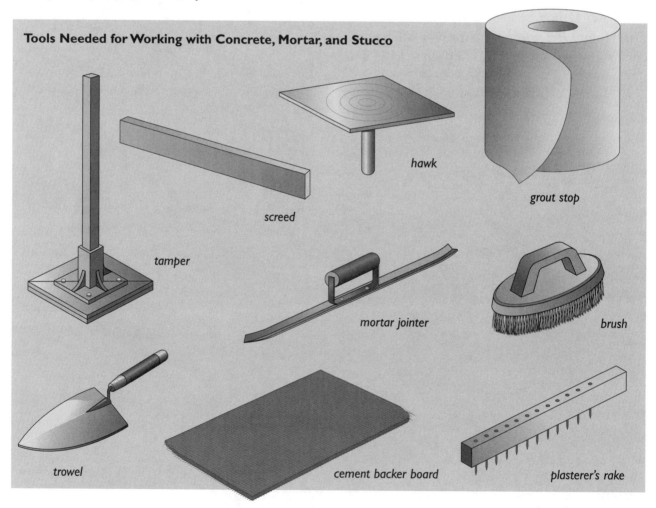

Tools Needed for Working with Concrete, Mortar, and Stucco

screed

hawk

grout stop

tamper

mortar jointer

brush

trowel

cement backer board

plasterer's rake

Materials

This is a basic primer on the materials used in the masonry trade. For more detailed information, consult a masonry construction book. Also, see *Material Specifications* (p. 22) and *Construction Procedures* (p. 23).

Concrete for the Footer

The basic ingredients of concrete are sand, coarse aggregate (crushed stone), portland cement, and water. The limestone in the cement reacts with the water in a process called hydration, which forms the concrete. You can mix your own concrete or, if you're going to need much more than a cubic yard, you may want to order it from a concrete company, who will deliver the materials directly to your construction site (make sure you know the exact quantity and have plenty of manpower available when it arrives, because concrete companies oftentimes charge not only by the load, but by the hour).

Calculating How Much You'll Need is a simple matter of multiplying the length of the footer (in feet) by the width by the depth and dividing by 27 feet to arrive at the number of cubic yards required. To avoid running short, estimate a little high (there's nothing worse or more inconvenient than to run out of concrete).

Mixing Your Own Concrete by Hand is a relatively simple procedure. In a wheelbarrow (or on a sheet of plywood), measure out equal amounts (one cubic foot each) of the dry ingredients in layers (coarse aggregate on the bottom, followed by the sand and then the cement). Mix these materials together thoroughly, using your mortar hoe. Then add a small amount of water (a gallon or less) and mix it together with the materials, again using your mortar hoe. Continue adding water and mixing it in until it's uniformly gray in color and shiny in appearance (but not soupy).

You can test the concrete by chopping the mixture with the blade of your mortar hoe. If the cuts made by your hoe are crumbly, add more water. If the cuts tend to soften and fill up, add more dry materials. If the mixture clings to the mason's hoe when pulled out of the concrete, the consistency is just right.

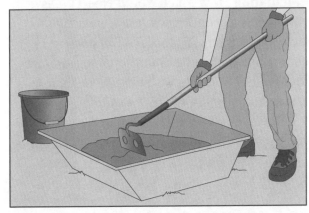

Mixing concrete by hand.

Using a Powered Concrete Mixer is just like mixing concrete by hand, only easier! With the mixer turned off, add the coarse aggregate and approximately half of the amount of water you'll need. Turn on the mixer and add cement and sand and the balance of the water. Test the concrete mix as described in the preceding paragraph. As soon as you're done, clean out the mixer by throwing in more gravel and water and turning it on for a few minutes. Complete the cleaning by hosing out the inside—otherwise, you'll have to chisel out the hardened cement.

Mortar

Mortar (the material used to bond together blocks, bricks, and stone) normally consists of approximately one part cement, four parts sand, and one-half part lime, all mixed together, with water added. Because of the size of the jobs contained in this book, I would buy bags of masonry cement mix rather than mixing your own ingredients.

Calculating How Much You'll Need is easy. One bag of masonry cement mix is enough to lay approximately 25 blocks or 100 bricks. As with concrete, mix the dry material together thoroughly in a wheelbarrow and then begin to mix in small amounts of water. Use your mortar hoe to test the readiness of the mixture in the same way you tested the concrete for the footer (another

way to test the consistency is to pick some up with your trowel and turn it upside down—if it sticks, great; but if it slides off, add more of the dry mix). Mix only enough mortar to last you for an hour or two.

Concrete Block

Block dimensions are always measured width × height × length. All the concrete blocks discussed here (except the cap block) contain hollow cores to save weight without sacrificing strength. These openings also allow for steel reinforcing rods (commonly known as rebar) to be installed which some of the designs in this book call for. There are several basic types of concrete blocks: *Stretcher Block* is the most common size of concrete block at 8"×8"×16" (it actually measures 7⅝"×7⅝"×15⅝", to which is added the normal mortar joint of ⅜"); *Half-stretcher Block* (8"×4"×16"); *Corner Block* (8"×8"×16"); *Cap Block* (8"×4"×16"); and *Four" Block* (8"×4"×16"). *End Blocks* come in the same dimensions, but have a smooth end.

Calculating How Much You'll Need is a matter of knowing how many of the 16" long blocks you'll need for one course times how many of the blocks (8 inches high each) it will take to reach the desired height. I've provided the exact number of blocks needed in the materials lists that accompany each of the designs in this book.

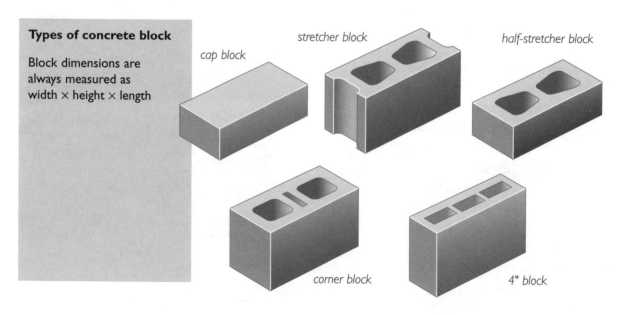

Types of concrete block

Block dimensions are always measured as width × height × length

cap block

stretcher block

half-stretcher block

corner block

4" block

Brick

There are two basic types of bricks that are used in this book: facing bricks and firebricks:

Face Bricks are used on the outside of walls and fireplaces. Face brick comes in many sizes, colors, and textures. Most face brick is made with holes for adhering purposes. If you live in a climate where there can be considerable freezing and thawing, be sure to use brick that can withstand the weather (check with your local supplier). There also is another alternative known as *Brick Veneer*, but it is used only for aesthetic purposes and *not for structural reasons*.

Firebricks are used in the construction of the hearths of fireplaces and barbecues, and are designed to withstand high temperatures. The standard size for firebrick is 4½"×2½"×9".

Calculating How Much You'll Need can be arrived at by dividing the square feet of the wall surface and dividing by seven, assuming an average brick with a face size of 2"×8" (double the number if you're building a wall two bricks thick). These figures are based on using a ⅜" joint. Bricks are usually less expensive if purchased in 500-brick lots (called *straps* because they're tied to a delivery pallet with steel straps). Because *straps* are usually 4' cubes weighing about a ton, have them delivered as close to your job site as possible.

Stone

If you want your project to blend into your surroundings, there is probably no better material to use than native stone. There are many types of stones, but the most common are *granite* (quite difficult to cut due to its hardness), *limestone* (easier to cut and saw and yet still strong), and *sandstone* (also quite easy to work with). The manner in which stone is gathered and prepared can be divided into two distinct categories: *quarried stone* (which is cut by machine) and *fieldstone* (which is collected in its natural form). Beyond that, there are three other categories of stone:

Rubble Stone is irregular round pieces of rock, and can either be fieldstone or left over from a quarrying operation. Because of its rustic appearance, its frequently used for building garden walls.

Ashlar Stone has been cut into fairly uniform, flat pieces, although the face of the stone can be left natural looking like rubble stone. It's often used for building walls and pathways.

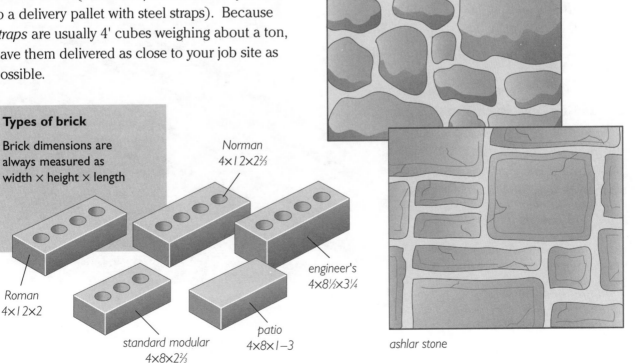

rubble stone

ashlar stone

Types of brick

Brick dimensions are always measured as width × height × length

Norman
4×12×2⅔

Roman
4×12×2

standard modular
4×8×2⅔

patio
4×8×1–3

engineer's
4×8½×3¼

Flagstone is stone (often limestone, slate, or shale) that is naturally flat and is an ideal (although expensive) paving material for patios and pathways and for the tops of benches and barbecue shelves.

Calculating How Much You'll Need is a little different from figuring out the number of concrete blocks or bricks. Stone is normally sold by the cubic yard. Simply multiply the length of the wall by its height and multiply that number by the width of the wall, and then divide that result by 27 to arrive at the number of cubic yards required. Be sure to add to the number to allow for breakage and for unusable stones.

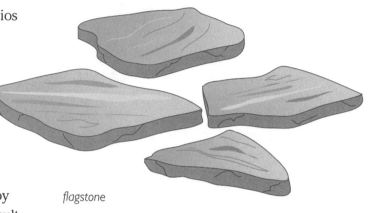

flagstone

Stucco

This is yet another alternative to facing stones and brick for the final surface of your project. Stucco is weather resistant and can be finished in a variety of textures. Stucco, however, is not advised for exterior finishes in the regions of the country that have freezing temperatures. Check with your local building codes and building suppliers before considering this finish. Stucco, which is generally applied in three layers for maximum durability, is a mortar consisting of 3 parts sand to 1 part portland cement and ¼ part lime with water added. Although it can be mixed at home, I recommend buying premixed stucco mix.

Calculating How Much You'll Need.
A 90-pound bag of premixed stucco covers 80 square feet using a ⅜" thickness. Coverage will vary depending upon thickness.

Rebar
The designs in this book call for #4 steel reinforcing rods (known as *rebars*) for extra strength. Rebars are placed in the footer as the concrete mixture is poured, and they extend up through the hollow cores of the concrete block as the structure is built. The cores containing rebar need to be filled with mortar to secure them.

rebar

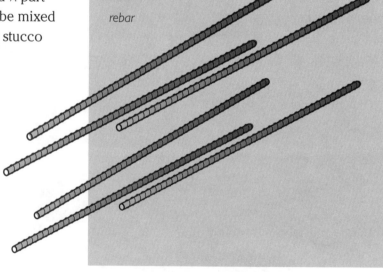

Building the Footer

The block walls of the structures shown in this book must be built on footers that extend to a depth below the frost or freeze line in your area in order to prevent the walls from cracking. Generally, footers must be twice as wide as the thickness of the wall you're going to build. While the plans in this book specify 24" footers (below grade unless otherwise specified), be sure to check your local building codes, which will dictate the depth and size of footers for your area.

Making the Forms

In areas where the soil is firm and compacted, it may be possible to avoid the forms altogether, using the trench itself as a form for the footer. Whether you use forms or not, be sure that the trench is deep enough so that the top of the footer will be at least 3" to 4" below the surface level of the finished grade.

Form Boards, Stakes, and Stretchers are

used to construct the forms for your footer. Place *form boards* (2×4s, 2×6s, or wider) on the edge to form the outline of your footer. Before moving on to the next step, check the form boards in all directions with a carpenter's level to make certain that the form is the same height all the way around (the top of your form will be the top of your footer). These are held in place by 1×4 *stakes* hammered into the ground every three or four feet and nailed to the form boards. (When building forms, use double-headed nails so you can easily remove them when you're done.) Every four or five feet, nail 1×4 *stretchers* across

the form to keep its width from shifting from the weight of the concrete you're going to pour into the forms. Use your carpenter's level again to check for uniformity of height.

Rebar to Reinforce the Footer may be required by your local building codes. To reinforce the footer, lay two lines of ½" rebar horizontally in the footer form, resting them on rebar holders or on scraps of 2×4s at least an inch or two from the sides of the form. To splice lengths of rebar together or to form corners where two lengths of rebar intersect, overlap the pieces by at least 12" and bind them together with 8-gauge wire. The plans and the materials lists in this book provide you with the amount of rebar to be used for your selected design.

Rebar to Reinforce the Wall of Your Structure may be indicated in the design plans for your particular project. Bend the rebar (you can rent a bending tool from tool rental agencies) into a 90-degree angle. Bind one side (at least 2" long) with 8-gauge wire to one of the horizontal lengths of rebar in your form. The upright arm of the new rebar should extend at least 18" above the top of the finished footer. Once you begin building the wall of your structure, you can tie on more vertical lengths of rebar that will run through the core of your concrete block. Again, the plans and material lists in this book provide you with the amount of rebar required for your selected design.

Pouring the Footer

This is as easy as mixing your own concrete or having it delivered and filling up your form. The concrete should come up to exactly the top of your form boards. Use a shovel or your mason's hoe to work through the concrete to release any trapped air bubbles. Then use a screed (a piece of 2×4 that is longer than the width of your form will do) to smooth the surface of the concrete. When the concrete hardens, cover it with plastic sheeting, and let the concrete cure for several days before proceeding with your project. When it's cured, remove the double-headed nails from the form and pry the boards away from the concrete.

Working with Block

All of the designs featured in this book are built with concrete blocks. Admittedly, this is hard work. Concrete blocks can weigh up to 50 pounds each, and building an entire wall or structure with concrete blocks can be hard on your back. There's no shame in asking for help or hiring somebody to do the job for you. If you decide to go ahead and do it yourself, please reread the *Safety First!* (p. 5) section in this book, and remember: *lift with your legs.*

Testing the First Row

Take your time at the beginning to be sure where the initial course of blocks will be placed, since they will determine every row after that. Without using mortar, begin by laying out the first course of concrete blocks on the footer. Start by placing a smooth-end block at one end of the row, and then (using ⅜" wood slats as dividers to represent the mortar) line up the blocks according to the design plans. When you're certain the alignment is precise, use a carpenter's pencil to mark the outside edge of the end blocks, running the pencil line to the edges of the footer. Snap a chalk line on either side of the row of blocks as a guide.

Laying the First Course

If the footer has cured for more than just a few days, wet it down lightly before proceeding. Using a trowel, place two 1" thick strips of mortar about three blocks long on one end of the footer. Place an end block (one that has a smooth end) into the mortar, and make sure it falls exactly within your pencil and chalk lines. Using the end of the trowel, tamp the block firmly into the mortar.

Using a Folding Rule, measure from the footer to the top of the block (it should be 8"). If it's too low, remove the block and use more mortar and then measure again. If it's too high, use your trowel and tamp the block down and then measure again. Use your carpenter's level to make sure the block is level.

Apply Mortar to the Ends of Two More Blocks and lay them next to your end block. Follow the same measuring instructions provided for the initial block (remember: the mortar between the blocks also needs to be ⅜" thick).

Repeat the Above Steps at the Other End to establish the outside lines of your structure. Next, pound 1×4 stakes into the ground beyond both ends and tie mason's cord to the stakes and stretch tautly. The cord should be exactly at the top of the blocks at both ends (use a line level to check).

Complete the First Course by working back and forth from either end until you reach the middle. Measure the distance between the last two blocks. If necessary, cut a block to fit in this gap (allowing for ⅜" bands of mortar at each end of the block). Apply mortar to the ends of this final block and insert into the gap.

filling block

Finish the Joints as you work by using a brush to remove excess mortar, and a mortar jointer to compact the mortar and apply a professional finish to the joints (do the vertical joints first, and then do the horizontal joints in one long, smooth stroke).

Laying the Second and Subsequent Courses

Repeat the same process used for the first row of blocks, remembering to measure and level as you go. Begin the second row with a half-sized end block in order to achieve the desired staggered pattern. If your wall has a corner, however, use a full-sized block on one wing of the wall placed across the end of the block on the other wing to achieve the same staggered effect.

Incorporating Curved Designs

Building a structure that deviates from a straight line is not all that different or difficult. You begin by laying out the first course dry (without mortar) until it matches the design plans, and then outlining the blocks with a grease pencil. The edges of the blocks closest to each other need to be ⅜" apart to allow for the mortar. Once the first few blocks are mortared into place, apply more mortar between the wider parts of the joint until all the spaces are filled. If you're building a curved wall, the second and subsequent courses of block are laid the same as the first.

Using Block in Building a Beehive Fireplace

Beehives are a bit trickier (but worth the extra effort!). Before building one of these dome-shaped fireplaces, you must build the hearth with firebricks and install the flue liner (see sections *Building the Hearth* [p. 21] and *Installing the Flue Liner* [p. 21]). Once those steps are completed, you can begin laying the first course of block (as described in the preceding paragraph). The second course (and subsequent courses) will need to be laid a bit off center from the preceding course (the plans in this book show the exact layout of each course of block for these curved designs). Following the plans for your structure, repeat these steps until you are finished. Use a template cut to the size of the curved opening for structural support while building your fireplace. Construct the template by using two pieces of ½" plywood connected in the middle with 2×4s (see illustration below).

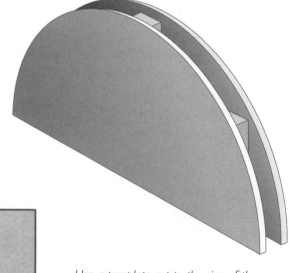

Use a template cut to the size of the curved opening for structural support while building your fireplace.

Laying the second and subsequent courses.

Finishing Techniques

Before you build your fireplace, barbecue, or bench, you should decide what kind of finish it's going to have: stone, brick, or stucco. If you plan to use a facing of either bricks or stone, you need to incorporate corrugated metal anchors (also known as *wall ties*) into the mortar between the concrete blocks (install them between every other course of block approximately 30" apart). Following are basic instructions involved in applying each of these three veneers to your structure.

Stone

A stone veneer is a less expensive way to achieve the look of a stone wall without having to use rocks to build the entire structure, but it does require that you install corrugated metal anchors in the mortar of your block wall (an alternative would be to apply metal lath, as described in *Stucco* below, and a ½" base of standard mortar). Use larger stones for the bottom course and lay them in mortar on the footer. Use stones of decreasing size and arrange them so that the joints are staggered as you work your way up. You can use natural stone for your veneer, or you can use cultured stone, which is often indistinguishable from the real thing. While the thickness of the mortar joint is not as critical as when laying concrete blocks or bricks, try and achieve a uniform width of approximately ⅜". Finish off the joints as you work by using a brush to remove excess mortar and a mortar jointer to compact the mortar and apply a professional finish to the joints (do the vertical joints first, and then do the horizontal joints in one long, smooth stroke).

Brick

A facing of brick is another option. Again, you'll need to plan ahead and have corrugated metal anchors imbedded in the mortar of your block wall. As with stone, lay the first course in mortar directly on the footer, starting with bricks at both ends and working your way toward the middle. As with block, a precise mortar thickness of ⅜" will provide you with professional results. Finish off the joints in the same manner as described in the preceding paragraph. If you plan on using veneer bricks, apply metal lath (see *Stucco*) and a ½" base of standard mortar in place of the corrugated metal anchors.

Stucco

A stucco exterior involves more steps, but allows you more room for creativity in finish designs and colors.

Attaching the Wire Lath is the first step. Using self-tapping masonry screws or masonry nails, anchor the lath directly to the concrete blocks. Use tin snips to cut the lath to fit around corners and curves.

Prepare the Stucco yourself or buy it premixed. Because it's not going to take all much stucco to cover the size of the projects in this book, I recommend buying premixed stucco mix in bags. However, if you're a purist and want to mix your own, here's the recipe: Mix three parts sand with one part portland cement and ¼ part lime and add just enough water so that a handful of the stucco holds its shape when you squeeze it into a ball and let go.

Apply the Scratch Coat of stucco over the metal lath using a trowel. This layer should be approximately ⅜" thick (to be certain of the depth, you can drive masonry nails in to the concrete block and tie mason's cord between the nails ⅜" out from the lath and build the stucco up to the height of the strings). Allow this coat to slightly set and then use a plasterer's rake to scratch the entire surface to a depth of approximately ⅛". This allow for greater adhesion when you apply the second coat. Allow two or three days for this scratch coat to cure, keeping it damp by spraying it lightly with a garden hose two or three times a day (a bit less if it's cloudy and humid, a bit more if it's sunny and dry).

The Brown Coat comes next. This extra coat of stucco (it, too, should be about ⅜" thick) greatly increases the strength of your stucco veneer. For the types of structures featured in the designs in this book, I highly recommend the little extra time and expense of applying the brown coat. As with the first coat, allow it to cure for two or three days and keep it damp.

Applying the Finish Coat of stucco, approximately ⅛" to ¼" thick. While it's still fresh, you can texture the surface in a variety of ways from smooth (keep going over the surface with the trowel until the stucco is even) to stippled (using the bristles of a brush or a broom, gently slap the surface of the stucco in different directions). Or you can simply use the trowel in sweeping motions to create the desired effect. You can even use a combination of these ideas. Let your imagination be your guide! Once you're done, cure this final coat over the next two or three days by keeping it damp. If you plan to paint the stucco, wait at least five to six weeks to allow the curing process to be complete.

first coat

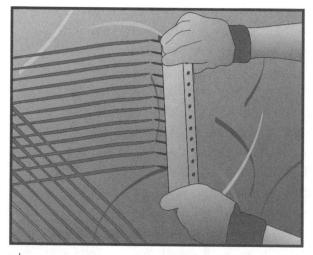

rake

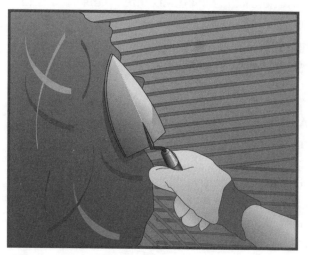

second coat

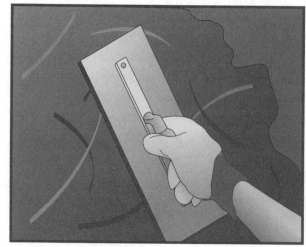

finish

More Information About Beehives, Fireplaces, Fire Pits, & Barbecues

Following are additional things you need to decide before beginning your project:

Installing a Gas Line and Adding Electricity

If you want to add either or both of these utilities to your project, you need to incorporate them into your plans from the very beginning. Several of the designs in this book can accommodate gas and electricity, but it is not recommended that you attempt to do this part of the project yourself. In fact, most building ordinances require that you get licensed professionals to do this work for you. The convenience of being able to flip a switch and have light and music in your outdoor entertainment area and of being able to turn a valve and have a fire in your fireplace or in your grill are distinct advantages (and ensure that you'll use and enjoy your outdoor areas more frequently).

Built-in Barbecues

There is a distinct richness to having a barbecue enclosed in masonry and finished off with stucco, brick, or stone. The dimensions in the designs included in this book are calculated to accommodate gas grills manufactured by Peterson's FireMagic. As the dimensions for grills made by other manufacturers are likely to be different (in fact, those for Peterson's FireMagic grills may change from time to time), be sure to get the exact dimensions and instructions for the grill you'll be installing.

Building the Hearth

Mark off area for hearth, keeping to 8" increments (*e.g.*, 24"×24") because of the size of firebricks. Excavate and level the ground for the footer. Evenly place rebar holders on the bottom of the footer and place rebar on holders (bending where needed). Overlap the ends of rebar and tie together with wire. Mark 8" up from the bottom of the footer and pour concrete to that depth, and let cure. Hand lay first course of concrete block (8×8×16), and make any necessary cuts to fit. Install that course, and then hand lay the second course (again, making any necessary cuts). Install the second course, which will bring you to grade level. Install two more courses (which will bring you to 16" above grade) and cap with whatever materials you have selected (tile, stone, brick). Because the hearth is built outside of the firebox, the firebrick is used inside the firebox.

Installing the Flue Liner

Because there are many different sizes of flue liners commonly used in building exterior fireplaces, be sure to refer to the "Materials List" for the design you select to build. Set the flue liner in mortar on top of the block and let it cure for 24 hours. Then follow the instructions for applying stucco provided in the *Finishing Touches* (p. 19) section of this book.

Material Specifications

All materials should comply with local building codes.

Concrete

All concrete shall be a minimum of 2500 psi compressive strength (approximately a 5 sack mix placed as a 4" (+/- 1") slump.

Reinforcing Steel

Reinforcing steel shall comply with ASTM A615, grade 40.

Masonry

Hollow concrete masonry units shall conform to ASTM C90, Grade N, Type I, fm = 1350 psi. Solid concrete masonry units shall conform to ASTM C145.

Grout

Grout in masonry walls shall develop 2000 psi compressive strength at 28 days.

Mortar

Mortar shall conform to ASTM C270, type M or S, and shall develop 1800 psi compressive strength at 28 days.

Structural Steel

All structural steel lintel angles shall be ASTM A-36.

Construction Procedures

Footers

Footers for all benches, barbecues, or other masonry shapes less than 8'–0" in height shall be a minimum of 8" thick and project 4" minimum beyond the face of the masonry. For shapes greater than 8'–0" in height, footer shall be 12" thick and project a minimum of 12" beyond the face of the masonry. Reinforce all footers with a minimum of #4 reinforcing bars at 12" on center in two directions at approximately 90° to each other. All reinforcing in footers shall be kept 3" clear from the bottom and sides of all footers. Bottoms of all footers shall be placed a minimum of $^{18}\!/_{24}$" below grade or as required by local conditions and codes, and founded on natural undisturbed soils or properly compacted fill materials. Geographic areas such as the southwest only require an 8" footer.

Stem Walls

Stem wall (base of wall below grade surface) shall be solid grouted masonry or concrete. Concrete is highly recommended for areas with freeze/thaw conditions. Provide vertical reinforcing bars through stem wall for all vertical bars as required by the Masonry Section below. In addition, provide a #4 reinforcing bar horizontally in the top of all stem walls. This horizontal bar shall be continuous around the full perimeter of the stem section according to plan.

Masonry

Vertical Reinforcing   Reinforce all masonry shapes with #4 reinforcing bars placed vertically in the center of the cells at a maximum spacing of four feet on center. In addition, place a #4 reinforcing bar vertically at each corner and at the jambs of all openings. If masonry shape is curved or circular, a minimum of four #4 bars shall be placed vertically at quarter joints of the shape, but not less than 48" apart measured on the curve. All vertical bars shall extend into the footer and have a 6" hook. Completely fill all reinforced cells grout per

the specifications. The above requirements pertain to the perimeter course of masonry only, and not necessarily to any in-fill masonry in the core of the shape.

Horizontal Reinforcing   Provide a #4 reinforcing bar in the top of all masonry in a minimum 8"×8" solid grouted section of masonry. This horizontal bar shall be continuous (or provide a 20" lap splice) around the full perimeter of the masonry shape. Where the masonry extends higher than 8 feet above the top of the footer, provide an additional #4 bar horizontal at 8 feet on center in the same 8"×8" solid grouted section of masonry. Provide #9 ladder type horizontal joint reinforcing in alternate courses (16" on center) in perimeter course of masonry. In circular shapes where joint reinforcing is not practical, provide a #4 (or two #3) horizontal 8"×8" solid grouted section of masonry at 4 feet on center instead of 8 feet on center.

Lintels

Provide steel angle lintels over all openings in the masonry. Size of steel angles shall be of sufficient size to adequately carry the weight of the masonry over the opening. Provide a minimum of 4" of bearing (more for larger openings) of the angles on the masonry on each side of the opening.

Concrete Cap

Concrete cap or cover over top of benches, barbecues, or other masonry shapes shall be 4" thick poured over a galvanized corrugated metal sheeting or a plywood form. These forms can be left in place. They should rest 1½" to 2" onto the masonry at the perimeter of the shape. Rebar dowels shall be hooked 12" minimum into the vertical cells with vertical reinforcing and lapped into concrete cap. Masonry should be grouted and cured at least one day before pouring the concrete cap. Provide #3 bars at 12" on center each way or #4 bars at 18" on center each way in the middle of the concrete cap.

Notes

Creating a beautiful home is a high artistic achievement: enjoying it is the art of living.

Without the private world of retreat we all become unbalanced creatures.

Tuscany with Banco Seat (page 48)

The simple style and the colors accented by the flagstone trim on this combination fireplace/barbecue grill create a beautiful and functional entertainment area.

Tuscany with Boncho Seat
(page 48)

(left) Corners can be problem areas but in this unique design, the pool seems to flow right into the fireplace.

Circle Bar & Grill (page 99)

(below) The circular design set in this spacious backyard sets the tone for entertainment at its best.

(above) The design of this chimney imparts a European flair and brings a little bit of Italy to this interior courtyard.

(above) **This construction went below grade on a flat piece of ground and created a wonderful feeling of privacy.**

Barbecue (page 90)

(right) This simple eight-foot barbecue and side burners offers yet another alternative to outdoor cooking.

Fire Pit (page 86)

(left) This boulder and stone aggregate firepit sets the stage for a unique spa area.

Even though this large fireplace is indoors, it was constructed using the same basic methods described in this book. The author built this fireplace in her own home using river rock, bringing a touch of the East coast to the Southwest.

Brick Beehive (page 79)

The use of adobe bricks on this fireplace (also shown on the cover of this book) provides a look of old Mexico. Note the detail in the arched opening and hearth area of this fireplace.

Beehive (page 26)

(above) A truly Southwestern feeling is achieved by this simple beehive fireplace.

Modified Santa Fe (page 66)

(above) This fireplace with its added ledge stone creates a distinctive look.

(above) The author built her spa and thirty-five foot lap pool next to an in-ground fire pit which at night creates a striking balance of fire and water.

Fire Pit (page 86)

(left) An above-ground fire pit is perfect for warmth, an added conversation area, and also for roasting marshmallows!

Barbecue (page 90)

(right) This easy-to-build barbecue is a great way to start
your outdoor entertainment
area. You can always add a
fireplace and benches later, if
you wish.

Santa Fe (page 59)

(above) The unfinished rear yard fireplace renders a casual and relaxing
atmosphere, awaiting the home and backyard to be painted.

(right) The author's fireplace is complete with a television and a barbecue grill. Travertine trim and an Italian Cantera stone mantel add a touch of simplicity to this patio.

This beehive shows how easily a design can be altered by adding different stone finishing surfaces. This one utilizes river rock, otherwise known as cobblestone.

L-shaped Barbecue (page 104)

Patio columns can create great areas in which to incorporate a barbecue grill, using what might otherwise be considered an obstacle.

Tuscany Entertainment Center (page 53)

This beautiful structure is nearing completion. When done, it will even have a television in the small opening to the left

This indoor fireplace still needs an acid wash and wet lacquer finish to bring out the beautiful natural colors in the stone. This fireplace makes a wonderful cornerpiece in this new home. Note the detail of the vertical cobblestone archway in the photo below.

Beehive (page 26)

This beehive is under construction and shown prior to attaching the metal lath and stucco.

The tile incorporated into this grill offers yet another look.

Tuscany with Boncho Seat
(page 48)

(above) Reminiscent of an Italian villa, this fireplace will fit in anywhere in the world.

Beehive (page 26)

(above and right) **The basic beehive fireplace fits easily into any backyard entertainment area.**

Barbecue with Serving/Bar Area
(page 95)

When finished, this grill with tile and stone will set off a great corner of this new home.

(left) A combination of travertine and stucco provides a natural balance of colors, setting the mood for the evening.

(left) The combination of Saltillo and Mexican tile has created a true south of the border feeling in this backyard.

(below) This fireplace/grill and decorative floor tile create the perfect atmosphere for a fiesta any time of day or night.

(left) This ornate beehive is set off by stucco and a colorful blend of unique tilework.

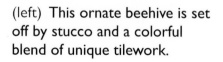

Fireplace and Barbecue Designs

Important Note

The design plans in this book are specifically drawn by the architect to accommodate natural gas/LP. If converting to wood burning, these plans would have to be redesigned by an architect or mason to accommodate firebox, flue, and chimney changes.

Also, the design plans in this book were drawn with 24" footers. Depending upon geographic location, consult your local building codes for depth requirements.

1. Beehive

Materials List

Concrete Blocks	180 (8×8×16) 220 (8×8×8) 20 (4×4×8)	**#4 Rebar**	2 pieces (18" long) 5 pieces (32" long)
Firebrick	100 (4½"×2½"×9")	**Rebar Holders**	40
Premix Concrete	50 (80-pound) bags	**12" Round Stake**	1
Premix Mortar	50 (75-pound) bags	**Metal Lath**	6 sheets (2'×8')
Premix Stucco	3 (90-pound) bags	**Flue Liner**	check with local masonry supply for size
#4 Rebar	3 pieces (20' long) 1 piece (15' long) 5 pieces (5' long) 5 pieces (4' long) 1 piece (40" long) 2 pieces (2' long)		

50 square feet of preselected material for hearth/seat (brick, flagstone, or tile)

Mason's Cord

Grease Pencil

INSTRUCTIONS

1. Mark center point, pound in stake

2. Using a 50" piece of mason's cord attached to the stake, draw a 100" diameter circle on the ground (this is the outside edge of the footer)

3. Using a 22" piece of mason's cord attached to the stake, draw a 44" diameter circle on the ground (this is the inside edge of the footer)

4. Mark rest of foundation for seating wall/hearth according to plan

5. Excavate and level the ground for footer

6. Mark wall for footer top with grease pencil to indicate where grade level block is to be placed

7. According to plan, place holders in two parallel rows on the floor of the excavation

8. According to plan, bend and place rebar in rebar holders

9. According to plan, overlap rebar and tie together with wire

10. Completely fill vertical rebar cells with concrete

11. Mix concrete and pour into footer

Step 2

Step 11

12. According to plan, hand lay first 2 courses of block below grade and then install them

13. According to plan, lay next two courses of block above grade

14. According to plan, backfill beehive firebox area to 4" from top course

15. Compact and level backfill

16. According to plan, place rebar holders in backfill

17. According to plan, place rebar (one 40" piece, two 2' pieces, and two 18" pieces) on the rebar holders

18. Mix and pour concrete

19. Hand lay first course of block (8×8×8) for beehive, make cuts if necessary, and then install the blocks (remember that the fireplace opening is 30")

20. In order to construct the curved opening of the beehive, place a template on top of hearth block. This will support the block work for the next 24 hours until the mortar sets around the arched opening

21. According to plan, hand lay two more courses of block (8×8×8)

22. According to plan, hand lay firebricks on floor, make cuts, and then install them

23. According to plan, hand lay firebricks on sides and back, make cuts as necessary

24. Continue to lay firebrick up to the top of the third course of the beehive

25. Using a masonry bit, drill a hole in the firebrick to accommodate the gas line (most fireplace gas lines are ½" inside diameter, so you will probably want to drill a 1" diameter hole)

Step 20

26. Backfill area between firebrick and outside wall with appropriate size block (or pieces of block)

27. According to plan, continue shaping beehive with two more courses of block (8×8×8). You will want to step back, look at your blockwork to make sure you are shaping the beehive symmetrically as you lay additional courses of block

28. Attach a 5' piece of rebar into blockwork with mortar

29. Build firebrick back wall to new course height

30. Continue backfilling with mortar using appropriate block size (the last course will be with 4x4x8 block using the 8" side vertically)

31. Continue shaping beehive with two more courses of block (8x8x8)

32. Only build two more courses of the firebrick wall

33. The last course on the beehive will be 4x4x8 block, with the 8" side vertical

34. Cap your fireplace with the 8" flue liner (brace the flue liner between the wall and the liner with 4x4x8 block set in mortar, making sure the top coat of mortar is slanted downward to allow the rain to run off) *(see illustration next page)*

35. Smooth and shape the beehive by attaching metal lath to the block with concrete nails/self-tapping screws

36. Once the lath is in place, the beehive is ready for the applications of stucco

37. Cut and install preselected hearth/seat material *(see illustration next page)*

38. Finish outside of beehive with preselected material, such as brick, flagstone, or tile *(see illustration next page)*

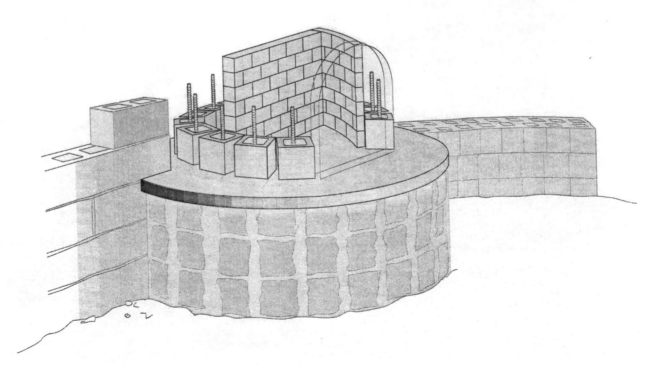

Step 29

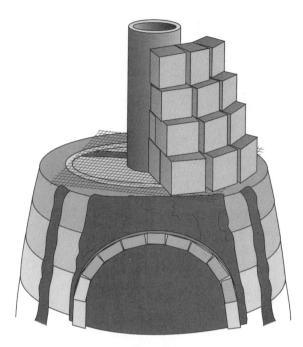

Step 34

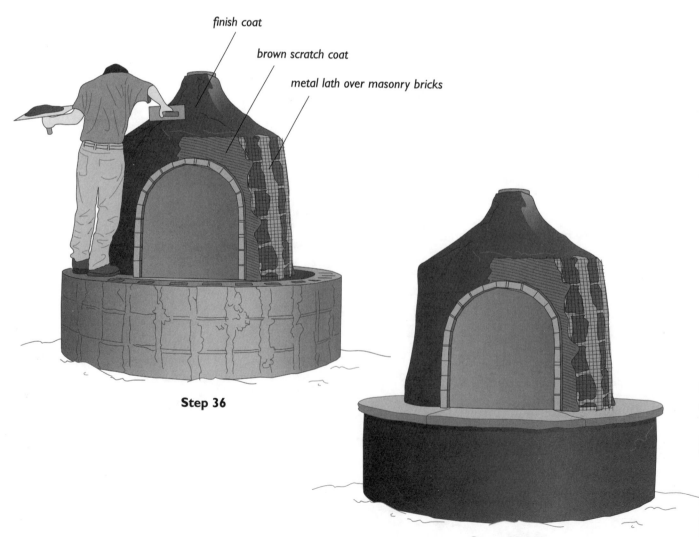

finish coat

brown scratch coat

metal lath over masonry bricks

Step 36

Steps 37-38

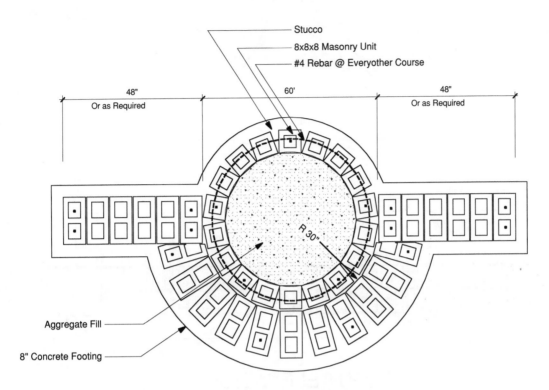

Stucco
8x8x8 Masonry Unit
#4 Rebar @ Everyother Course

48"
Or as Required

60'

48"
Or as Required

R 30"

Aggregate Fill

8" Concrete Footing

FOUNDATION PLAN

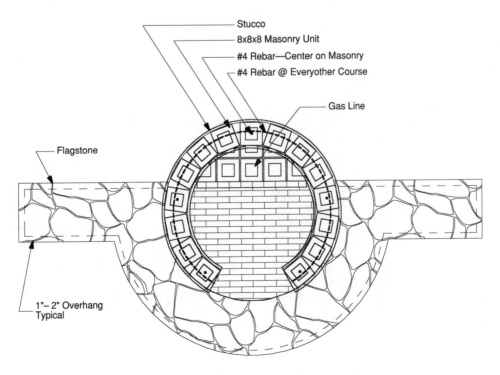

Stucco
8x8x8 Masonry Unit
#4 Rebar—Center on Masonry
#4 Rebar @ Everyother Course

Gas Line

Flagstone

1"– 2" Overhang
Typical

HEARTH PLAN

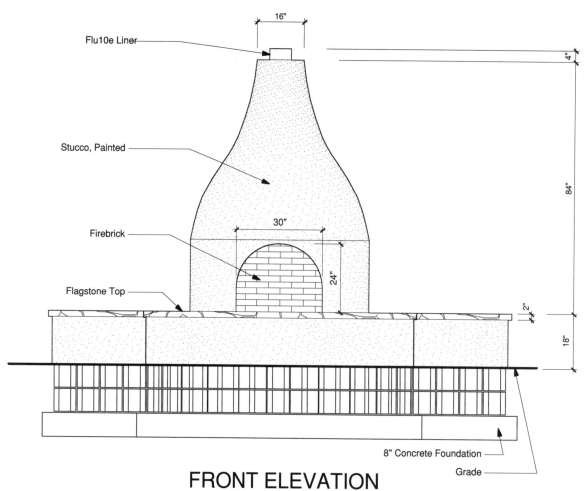

16"

Flu10e Liner

Stucco, Painted

30"

Firebrick

24"

Flagstone Top

84"

4"

2"

18"

8" Concrete Foundation

Grade

FRONT ELEVATION

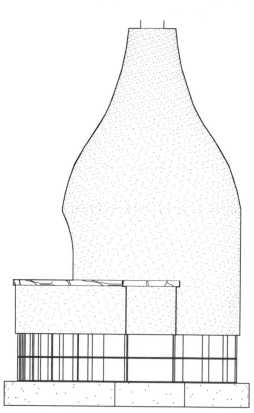

SIDE ELEVATION

I. Beehive

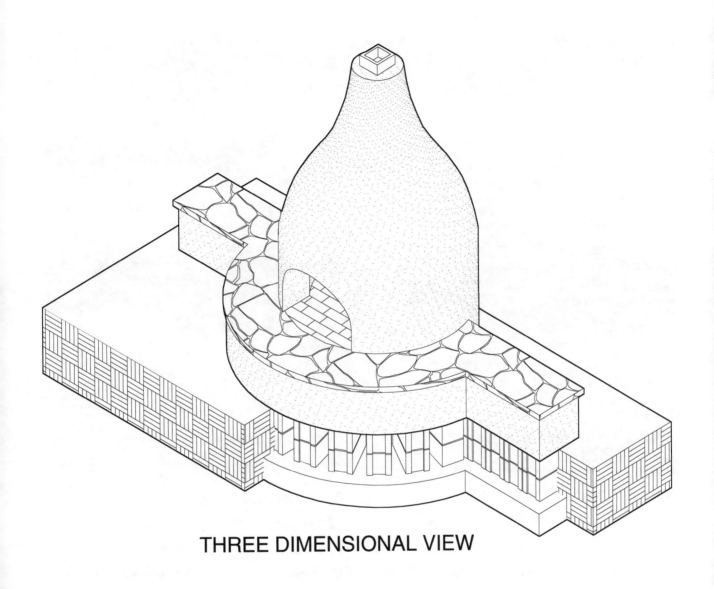

THREE DIMENSIONAL VIEW

Materials List

Concrete Blocks	400 (8×8×16) 130 (8×8×8) 75 (4×8×16) 30 (4×8×8) 25 (8×2×16) 12 (2×4×16)	**Rebar Holders**	50
		12" Round Stake	1
		Metal Lath	6 sheets (2'×8')
		8" Lintel	1 (8" longer than length of door—the size is determined by the builder/owner)
Firebrick	300 (4½"×2½"× 9")		
Premix Concrete	85 (80-pound) bags	**Cement Backer Board**	2 pieces (½"×3'×5')
Premix Mortar	60 (75-pound) bags		
Premix Stucco	5 (90-pound) bags	**Flue Liner**	check with local masonry supply for size
#4 Rebar	3 pieces (20' long) 1 piece (16' long) 5 pieces (6' long) 3 pieces (66" long) 12 pieces (5' long) 21 pieces (32" long)		

70 square feet countertop/hearth top material (brick, flagstone, or tile)

Barbecue unit and accessories

Mason's Cord

Grease Pencil

1. To lay out form for a beehive fireplace, measure 134" from the right edge of footer to the left, and 34" to front from the back edge of footer

2. Mark center point, and pound in stake

3. Using a 50" piece of mason's cord attached to the stake, draw a 100" diameter circle on the ground (this is the outside edge of the curved footer), and then measure and mark the rest of footer

4. Excavate and level the ground for footer

5. Mark the wall for footer top with grease pencil to indicate where the grade level block is to be placed

6. According to plan, place rebar on rebar holders

7. Shorten cord to 30" and draw a 60" diameter circle on the ground (this is the outside wall of the beehive)

8. Shorten cord again, this time to 22" and draw a 44" diameter circle on the ground (this is the inside wall)

9. Center the opening of the beehive at 30"

10. According to plan, determine four rebar locations by hand laying five blocks (8×8×8) on each side

11. Place the rebar holders in two parallel rows on the floor of the excavation

12. According to plan, take three pieces of the 20' rebar, one piece of the 16' rebar, and four pieces of the 6' rebar, bending them as necessary to overlap each other, tying them together with wire, and placing them on the rebar holders

13. According to plan, place vertical rebar along back raised wall

14. Mix concrete and pour into footer (since this is quite a bit of concrete, you may want to rent a portable concrete mixer or call a concrete company)

15. According to plan, from the center of the beehive, hand lay 10 blocks (8×8×8) on equal sides in between the previously marked arcs (be sure that the blocks fit over the vertical rebar—the open distance from end to end of the beehive mouth should be 30")

16. According to plan, inside the beehive, hand lay blocks (8×8×8) next to the first raised wall, from side to side of the beehive's first course

17. According to plan, hand lay firebricks on floor, make cuts and then install them

18. Using a masonry bit, drill a hole in the firebrick to accommodate the gas line (most fireplace gas lines are ½" inside diameter, so you'll probably want to drill a 1" diameter hole)

19. According to plan, making necessary cuts in the block, set first, second, third, and fourth courses (make sure to install access door and barbecue grill when laying courses)

20. Following the directions in Beehive #1, but using the dimensions for design #2, finish firebrick template area up to third course of Beehive

21. According to plan, continue your block work making any necessary cuts and following through for the raised wall area

22. Note: To build the two shelves, it will be necessary to mark an equal distance from beehive and cut block (make width of shelf 8")

23. According to plan, install additional vertical rebar to existing rebar (overlap at least 8" to 10" and tie together with wire); in continuing the chimney and downsizing your block size up to the flue liner, your vertical rebar must be curved inward to stay in the block cells

24. Step back and examine the shape and continue with courses according to plan (as your beehive takes shape, you should be near the seventh course)

25. Completely fill all rebar with concrete

26. By your ninth course, your rebar will now set in between block and mortar joint

27. Completely fill all block cells on the last course with concrete

28. Following instructions on Beehive #1, install flue liner, metal lath, and stucco for barbecue and fireplace areas

29. Horizontally, across the top of barbecue area, cut and fit backer board, and install with mortar

30. Finish seat and hearth areas with preselected materials and install and hook up barbecue grill

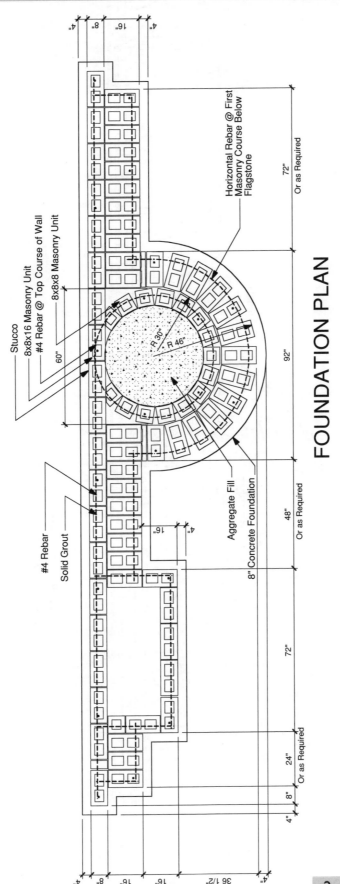

FOUNDATION PLAN

Stucco
8x8x16 Masonry Unit
#4 Rebar @ Top Course of Wall
8x8x8 Masonry Unit

Horizontal Rebar @ First
Masonry Course Below
Flagstone

#4 Rebar
Solid Grout

Aggregate Fill
8" Concrete Foundation

R 30"
R 46"

60"

72"
Or as Required

92"

48"
Or as Required

72"

24"
Or as Required

8"

4"

4"
8"
16"
4"

16"
4"

16"
16"
36 1/2"
4"
8"

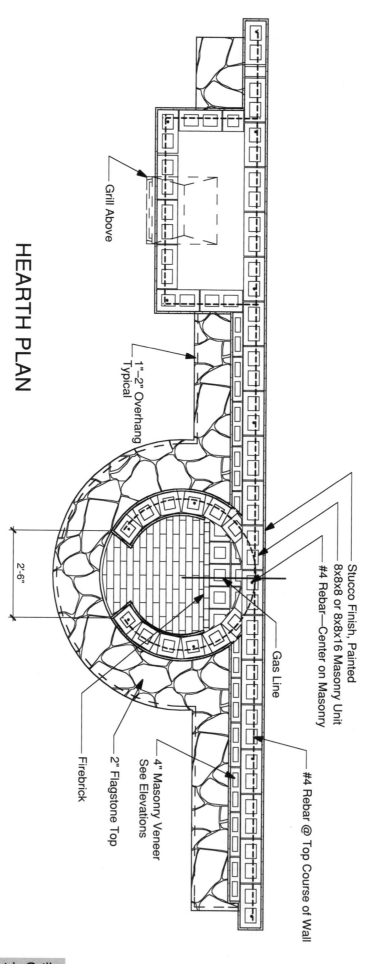

HEARTH PLAN

Grill Above

1"–2" Overhang
Typical

2'-6"

Stucco Finish, Painted
8x8x8 or 8x8x16 Masonry Unit
#4 Rebar—Center on Masonry

Gas Line

Firebrick

2" Flagstone Top

4" Masonry Veneer
See Elevations

#4 Rebar @ Top Course of Wall

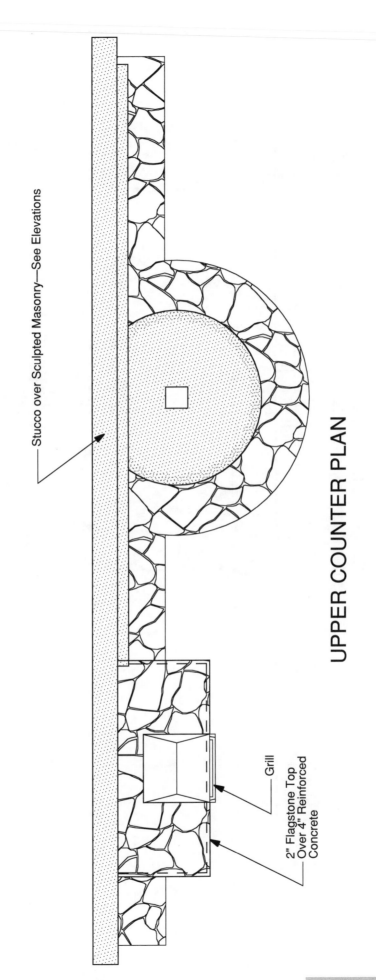

Stucco over Sculpted Masonry—See Elevations

Grill

2" Flagstone Top Over 4" Reinforced Concrete

UPPER COUNTER PLAN

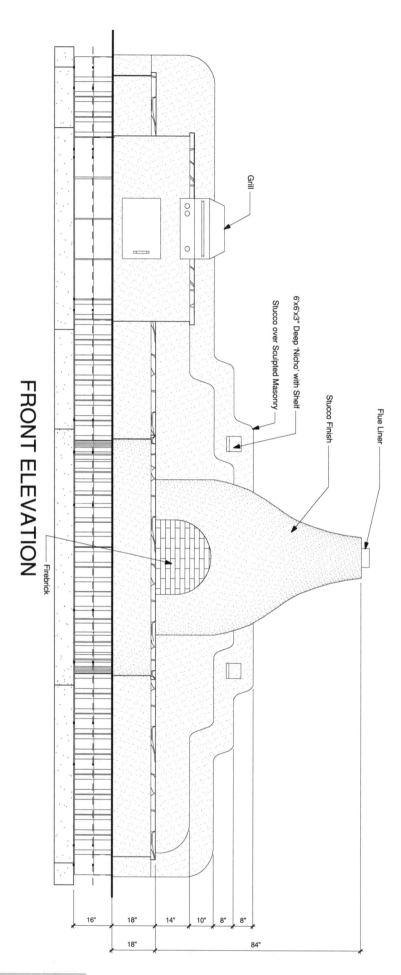

FRONT ELEVATION

Grill

6"x6"x3" Deep 'Nicho' with Shelf

Stucco over Sculpted Masonry

Stucco Finish

Flue Liner

Firebrick

16" 18" 14" 10" 8" 8"

18" 84"

40   2. Beehive with Grill

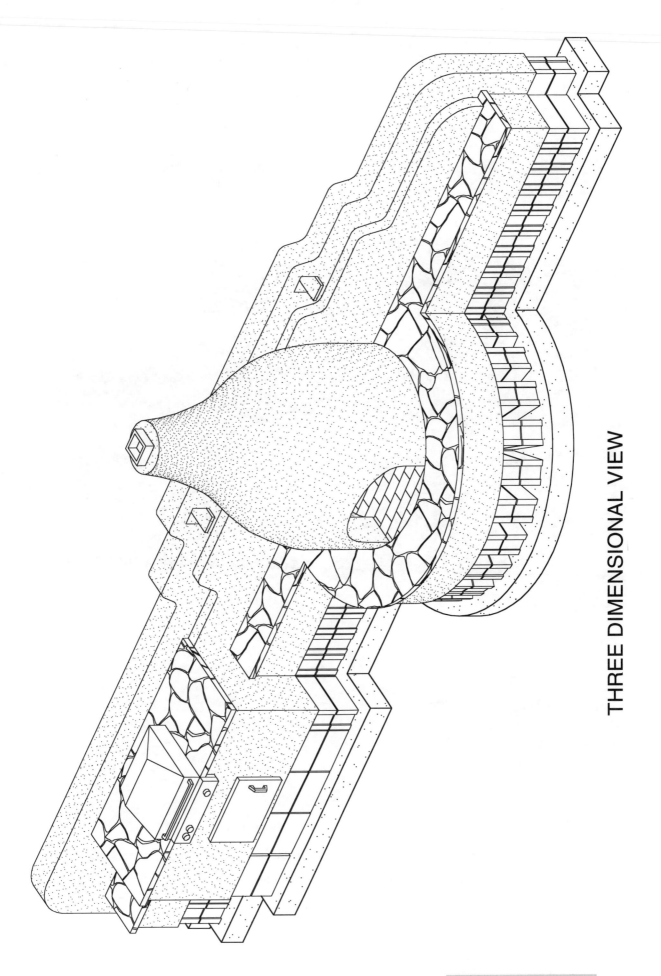

THREE DIMENSIONAL VIEW

3. Tuscany

Materials List

Concrete Blocks	120 (8x8x16)	**#4 Rebar**	2 pieces (15' long)
	20 (8x4x16)		4 pieces (5' long)
	10 (4x8x16)		3 pieces (4' long)
	20 (4x8x8)		6 pieces (32" long)
Firebricks	100	**Rebar Holders**	12
Premix Concrete	25 (80-pound) bags	**Metal Lath**	2 pieces (2'x8')
Premix Mortar	50 (75-pound) bags	**Flue Liner**	check with local masonry supply for size
Premix	3 (90-pound) bags		
		Grease Pencil	

INSTRUCTIONS

1. According to plan, mark outside edge of foundation

2. Excavate and level the ground for footer

3. Mark the wall for top of footer with grease pencil to indicate where the grade level block is to be placed

4. According to plan, place rebar vertically in the corners and then backfill

5. According to plan, place rebar holders on the floor of the excavation

6. According to plan, bend and place the rebar in rebar holders

7. According to plan, overlap and wire tie necessary rebar

8. Completely fill vertical rebar cells with concrete

9. Mix concrete and pour into footer

10. According to plan, hand lay first two courses of block below grade and then install them

11. According to plan, hand lay two courses of block above grade and then install them

12. According to plan, place the balance of rebar in rebar holders, advancing you to the second course

13. According to plan, lay third course of block, leaving 32" for fireplace opening

14. Place template on top of third course

15. According to plan, repeat prior instructions for installing firebrick as in Beehive #1, making note of the slanted firebrick roof

16. Backfill area between firebrick and outside wall with appropriate size block or pieces of block

17. Using a piece of cut plywood and 2×4s for support, angle back vertical wall to angled roof

18. According to plan, continue on courses, making cuts with masonry saw or chisel to shape throat of chimney

19. According to plan, install flue liners with mortar, reaching the final flue liner on top

20. Continue building block on outside to reach the top, exposing the flue liner

21. Following instructions and materials list for Beehive #1, install metal lath, brick, flagstone, and tile

22. Finish stucco

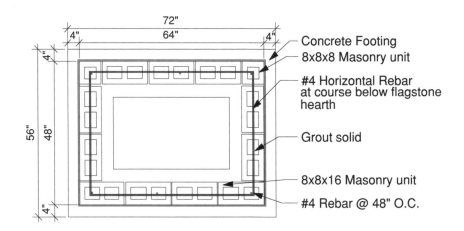

Concrete Footing
8x8x8 Masonry unit

#4 Horizontal Rebar
at course below flagstone
hearth

Grout solid

8x8x16 Masonry unit
#4 Rebar @ 48" O.C.

FOUNDATION PLAN

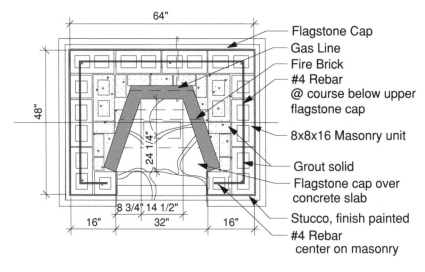

Flagstone Cap
Gas Line
Fire Brick
#4 Rebar
@ course below upper
flagstone cap

8x8x16 Masonry unit

Grout solid
Flagstone cap over
concrete slab

Stucco, finish painted

#4 Rebar
center on masonry

HEARTH PLAN

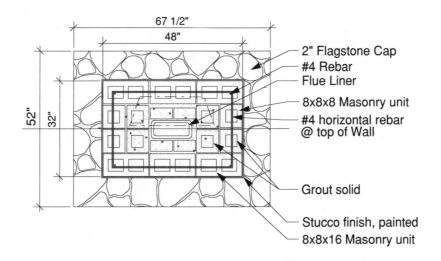

67 1/2"
48"
52"
32"

2" Flagstone Cap
#4 Rebar
Flue Liner
8x8x8 Masonry unit
#4 horizontal rebar @ top of Wall
Grout solid
Stucco finish, painted
8x8x16 Masonry unit

UPPER CHIMNEY PLAN

0   1   3   6

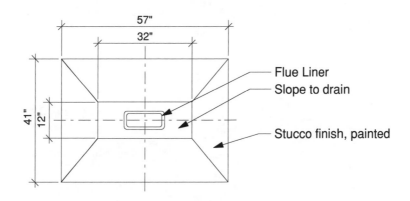

57"
32"
41"
12"

Flue Liner
Slope to drain
Stucco finish, painted

CHIMNEY CAP PLAN

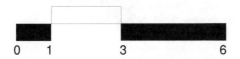

0   1   3   6

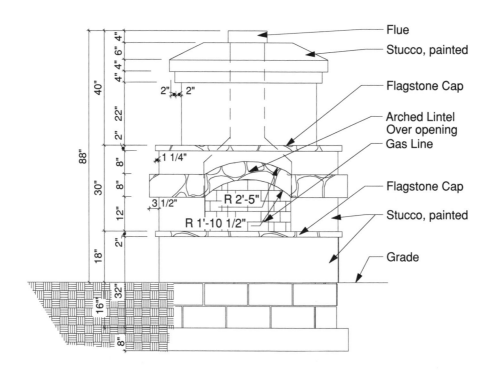

FRONT ELEVATION

0   1   3   6

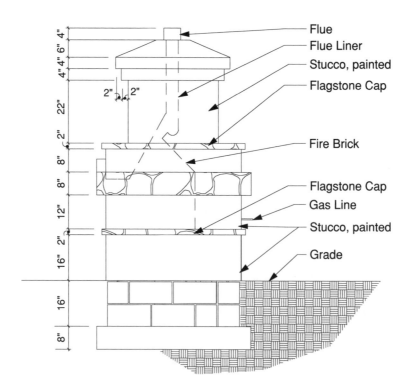

RIGHT SIDE VIEW

0   1   3   6

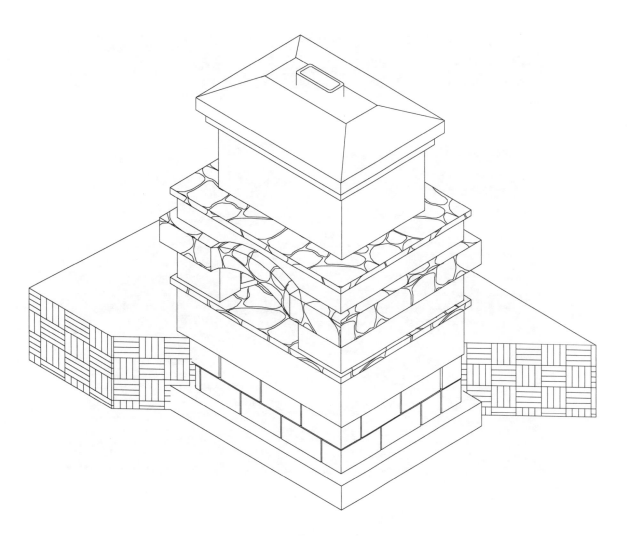

THREE DIMENSIONAL VIEW

4. Tuscany with Banco Seat

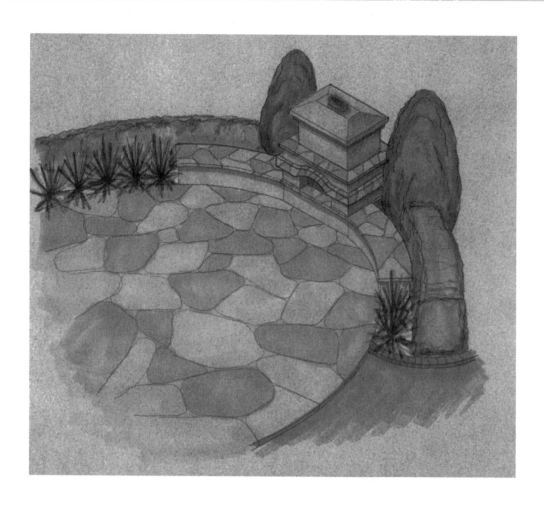

Materials List

Concrete Blocks	40 (8×8×16)	#4 Rebar	4 pieces (8' long)
	4 (8×8×8)		2 pieces (4' long)
	4 (4×8×16)		7 pieces (32" long)
Firebricks	100	Rebar Holders	6
Premix Concrete	35 (80-pound) bags	Flue Liner	check with local masonry
Premix Mortar	75 (75-pound) bags		supply for size
Premix Stucco	2 (90-pound) bag		

40 square feet of additional surface tops

60 square feet of surface wall finish

Instructions

This design will be built the same way as the previous Tuscany #3 design, except the foundation for this structure requires additional materials (listed above) to accommodate the added seating areas. (See plan for changes.)

CONSTRUCTION PLANS

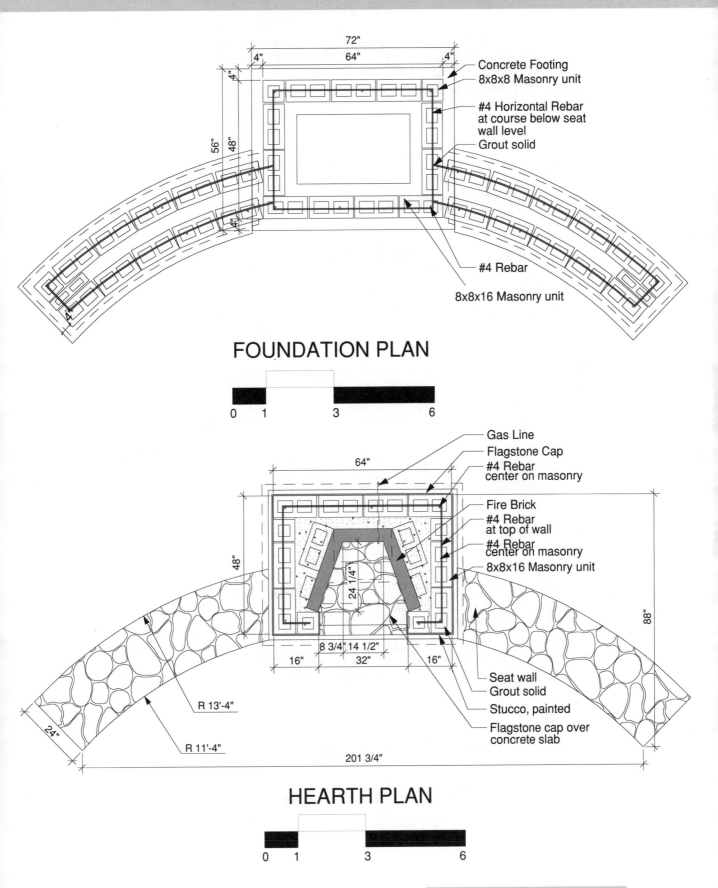

FOUNDATION PLAN

72"
64"
4"
4"
4"
56"
48"
4"
4"

Concrete Footing
8x8x8 Masonry unit

#4 Horizontal Rebar
at course below seat
wall level
Grout solid

#4 Rebar

8x8x16 Masonry unit

0   1   3   6

Gas Line
Flagstone Cap
#4 Rebar
center on masonry

64"

Fire Brick
#4 Rebar
at top of wall
#4 Rebar
center on masonry
8x8x16 Masonry unit

48"
24 1/4"
88"

8 3/4" 14 1/2"
16"   32"   16"

R 13'-4"
24"
R 11'-4"
201 3/4"

Seat wall
Grout solid
Stucco, painted
Flagstone cap over
concrete slab

HEARTH PLAN

0   1   3   6

4. Tuscany with Banco Seat   49

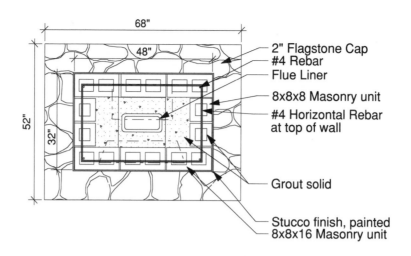

Labels for Upper Chimney Plan:
- 2" Flagstone Cap
- #4 Rebar
- Flue Liner
- 8x8x8 Masonry unit
- #4 Horizontal Rebar at top of wall
- Grout solid
- Stucco finish, painted
- 8x8x16 Masonry unit

Dimensions: 68", 48", 52", 32"

UPPER CHIMNEY PLAN

0   1   3   6

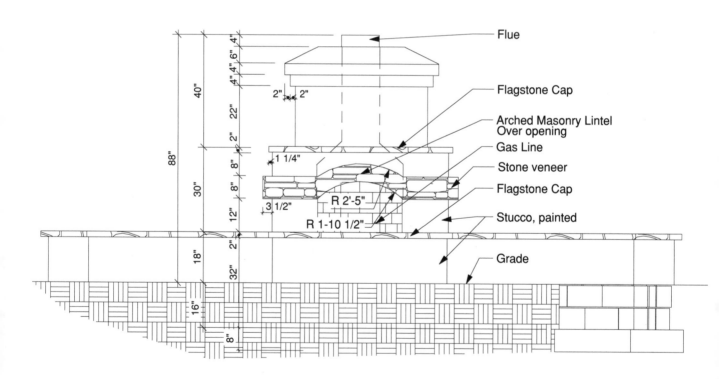

Labels for Front Elevation:
- Flue
- Flagstone Cap
- Arched Masonry Lintel Over opening
- Gas Line
- Stone veneer
- Flagstone Cap
- Stucco, painted
- Grade

Dimensions: 4", 4", 4", 6", 2", 2", 22", 2", 1 1/4", 8", 8", 3 1/2", 12", R 2'-5", R 1-10 1/2", 2", 18", 32", 16", 8", 40", 30", 88"

FRONT ELEVATION

0   1   3   6

4. Tuscany with Banco Seat

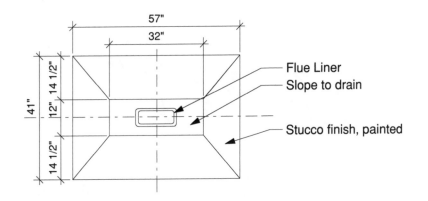

CHIMNEY CAP PLAN

Flue Liner
Slope to drain
Stucco finish, painted

57"
32"
41"
14 1/2"
12"
14 1/2"

0   1   3   6

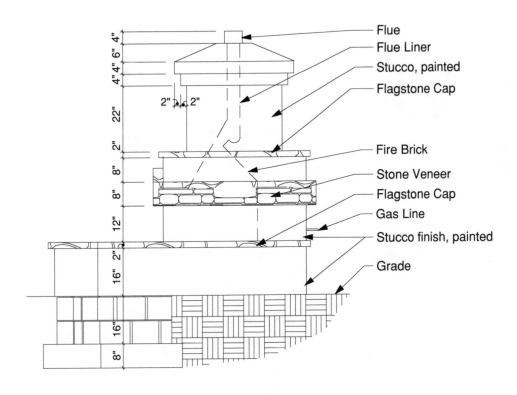

Flue
Flue Liner
Stucco, painted
Flagstone Cap

Fire Brick
Stone Veneer
Flagstone Cap
Gas Line
Stucco finish, painted
Grade

4"
4"
6"
4"
4"
22"
2"
8"
8"
12"
2"
16"
16"
8"

2" 2"

RIGHT SIDE ELEVATION

0   1   3   6

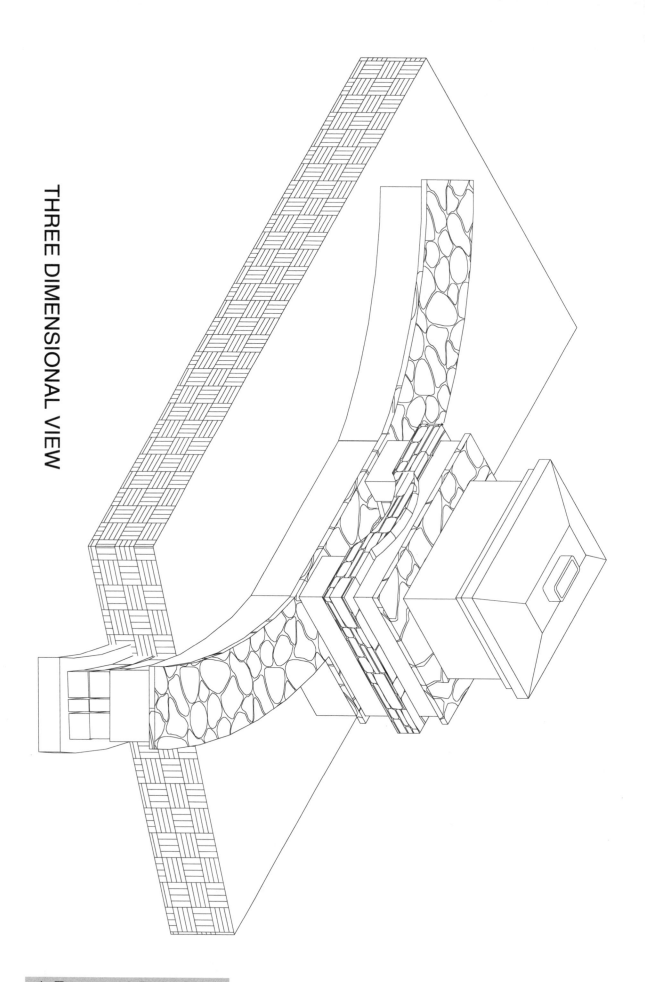

4. Tuscany with Banco Seat

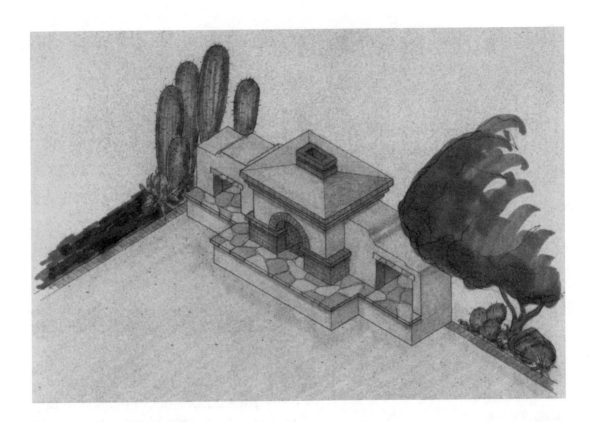

Materials List

Concrete Blocks	250 (8×8×16)
	40 (8×8×8)
	30 (8×4×16)
	50 (4×8×16)
Firebricks	100
Premix Concrete	60 (80-pound) bags
Premix Mortar	75 (75-pound) bags
Premix Stucco	3 (90-pound) bags
#4 Rebar	4 pieces (20' long)
	6 pieces (54" long)
	2 pieces (4' long)
	20 pieces (32" long)
Rebar Holders	45
Flue Liner	check with local masonry supply for size
Wooden Beams	2
Metal Lath	4 pieces (2'×8')
Cement Backer Board	2 pieces (½"×3'×5')
Electrical Conduit	Amount needed to cover distance from power source to entertainment center
GFIC Duplex Outlets	2

30 square feet of finishing material for hearth and seating

220 square feet of finishing material for exterior walls

Grease Pencil

INSTRUCTIONS

1. According to plan, mark outside edge of foundation

2. Excavate and level the ground for footer

3. Mark the wall for top of footer with grease pencil to indicate where the grade level block is to be placed

4. According to plan, have licensed electrician/plumber at this time add sleeve to accommodate electrical changes

5. According to plan, place rebar holder on the floor of the excavation

6. According to plan, bend and place rebar in rebar holders

7. According to plan, overlap and wire tie necessary rebar

8. Completely fill vertical rebar cells with concrete

9. Mix concrete and pour into footer

10. According to plan, hand lay appropriate courses of block to bring you to firebrick level

11. According to plan, set in template

12. According to plan, repeat instructions on firebrick from design #3 Tuscany

13. Backfill area between fireplace and firebox with appropriate size block or pieces of block

14. According to plan, at the fourth course, place wood beams on block, making any necessary cuts

15. According to plan, continue building firebrick area and block courses

16. Backfill any space between wall and firebox with appropriate size block or block pieces

17. According to plan, attach veneer on outside courses leaving room on outer edge for cap

18. Attach flue liner to block and mortar, continue with block courses making cuts as necessary

19. According to plan on Beehive #1, install metal lath and finish stucco

20. Install facing on corbel (the section directly above where the roof begins and has different levels projecting out from the structure) and on exterior veneer of fireplace

21. Install seat/hearth areas with preselected materials (brick, flagstone, tile)

CONSTRUCTION PLANS

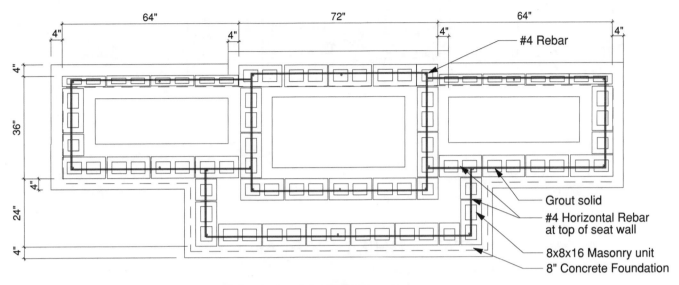

FOUNDATION PLAN

- #4 Rebar
- Grout solid
- #4 Horizontal Rebar at top of seat wall
- 8x8x16 Masonry unit
- 8" Concrete Foundation

0 1   3   6

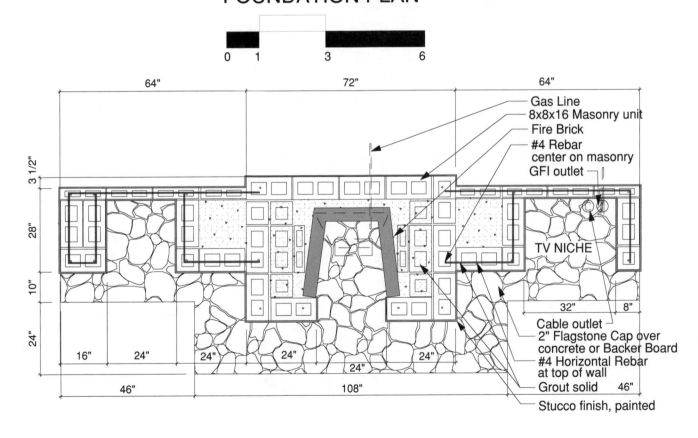

SEAT / FIRE BOX PLAN

- Gas Line
- 8x8x16 Masonry unit
- Fire Brick
- #4 Rebar center on masonry
- GFI outlet
- TV NICHE
- Cable outlet
- 2" Flagstone Cap over concrete or Backer Board
- #4 Horizontal Rebar at top of wall
- Grout solid
- Stucco finish, painted

0 1   3   6

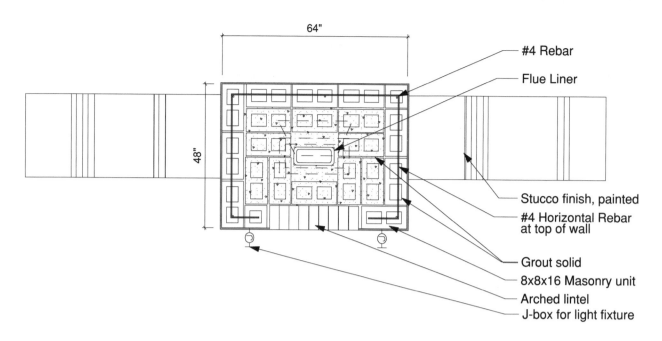

64"

48"

#4 Rebar

Flue Liner

Stucco finish, painted

#4 Horizontal Rebar
at top of wall

Grout solid

8x8x16 Masonry unit

Arched lintel

J-box for light fixture

LOWER CHIMNEY PLAN

0   1   3   6

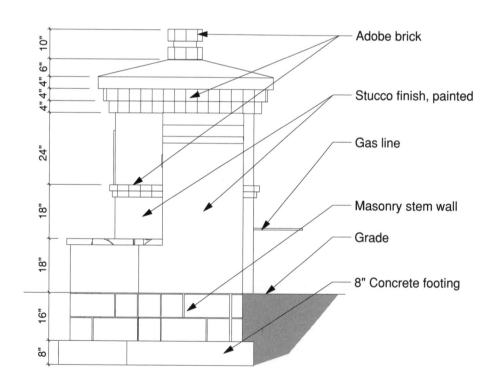

10"
6"
4" 4"

24"

18"

18"

16"

8"

Adobe brick

Stucco finish, painted

Gas line

Masonry stem wall

Grade

8" Concrete footing

RIGHT SIDE ELEVATION

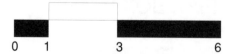

0   1   3   6

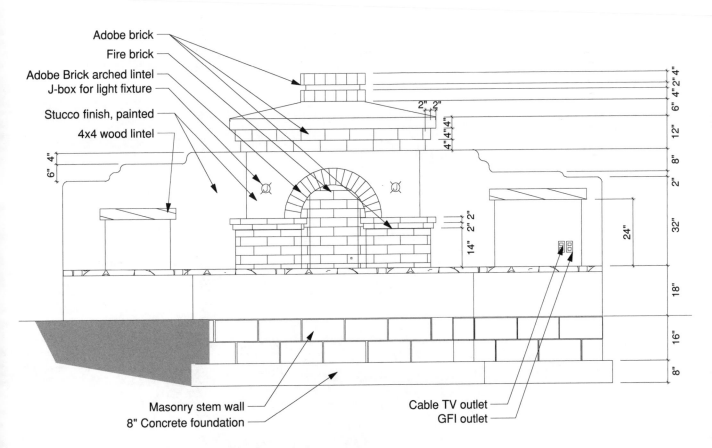

Adobe brick
Fire brick
Adobe Brick arched lintel
J-box for light fixture
Stucco finish, painted
4x4 wood lintel

2" 4"
4" 2" 4"
6"
12"
8"
2"
32"
24"
18"
16"
8"

2" 2"
4" 4" 4"
6" 4"
14" 2" 2"

Masonry stem wall
8" Concrete foundation

Cable TV outlet
GFI outlet

FRONT ELEVATION

0   1   3   6

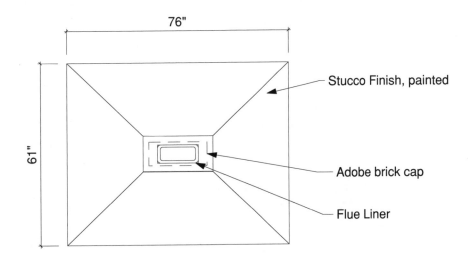

76"

61"

Stucco Finish, painted

Adobe brick cap

Flue Liner

UPPER CHIMNEY PLAN

0   1   3   6

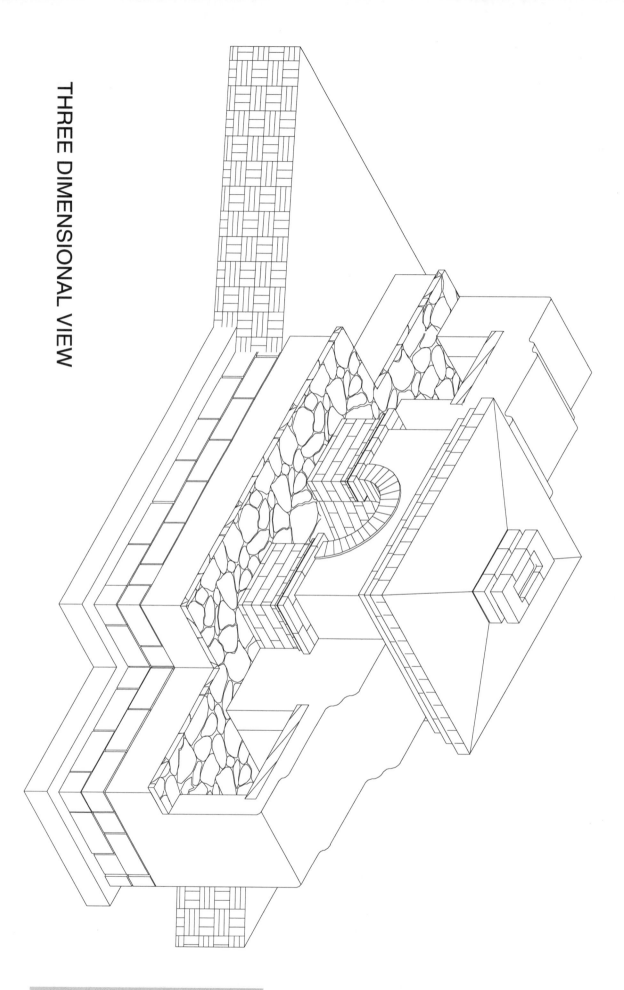

THREE DIMENSIONAL VIEW

5. Tuscany Entertainment Center

Materials List

Concrete Blocks	230 (8×8×16) 28 (8×8×8) 46 (4×8×16) 8 (4×8×8) 15 (8×4×16)	Rebar Holders	30
		Metal Lath	4 pieces (2'×8')
Firebricks	100	Cement Backer Board	4 pieces (½"×3'×5')
Premix Concrete	70 (80-pound) bags	Flue Liner	check with local masonry supply for size
Premix Mortar	60 (75-pound) bags		
Premix Stucco	3 (90-pound) bags		
#4 Rebar	3 pieces (20' long) 1 piece (10' long) 5 pieces (4' long) 27 pieces (32" long)		

50 square feet of finishing material for hearth and seating

200 square feet of finishing material for exterior walls

Grease Pencil

INSTRUCTIONS

1. According to plan, mark outside edge of foundation

2. Excavate and level the ground for footer

3. Mark the wall for top of footer with grease pencil to indicate where the grade level block is to be placed

4. According to plan, place rebar holders on the floor of the excavation

5. According to plan, bend and place rebar in rebar holders

6. According to plan, overlap and wire tie necessary rebar

7. Completely fill vertical rebar cells with concrete

8. Mix concrete and pour into footer

9. According to plan, hand lay two courses of block below grade and then install them

10. According to plan, hand lay appropriate courses to bring you to firebrick level

11. According to plan, set in template

12. According to plan, repeat instructions from design #3 Tuscany

13. Backfill area between fireplace and firebox with block or appropriate size pieces of block

14. Using appropriate block sizes, shape outside of fireplace to approximate contour as shown in architectural landscape drawing

15. Attach flue liner to block and mortar continuing with block courses around flu liner, making cuts as necessary

16. According to plan of Beehive #1, install metal lath and finish stucco

17. Install seat/hearth areas with preselected materials (brick, flagstone, tile)

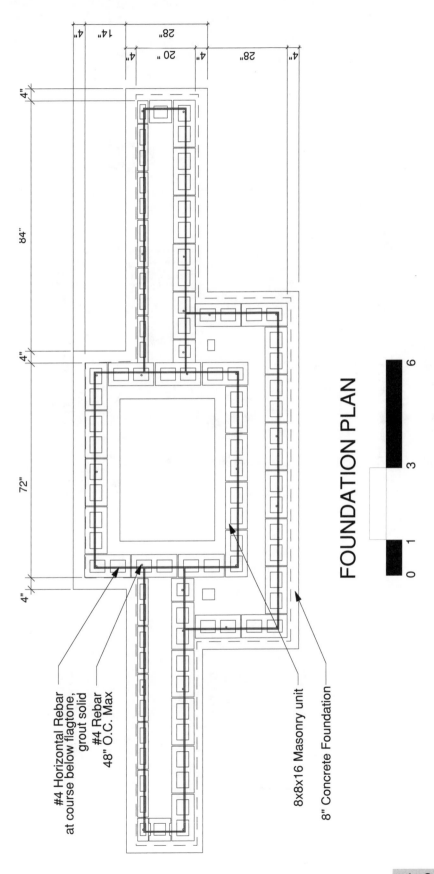

FOUNDATION PLAN

0   1   3   6

#4 Horizontal Rebar
at course below flagtone,
grout solid

#4 Rebar
48" O.C. Max

8x8x16 Masonry unit

8" Concrete Foundation

4" 14" 28"

4" 20" 4" 28" 4"

4"

84"

4"

72"

4"

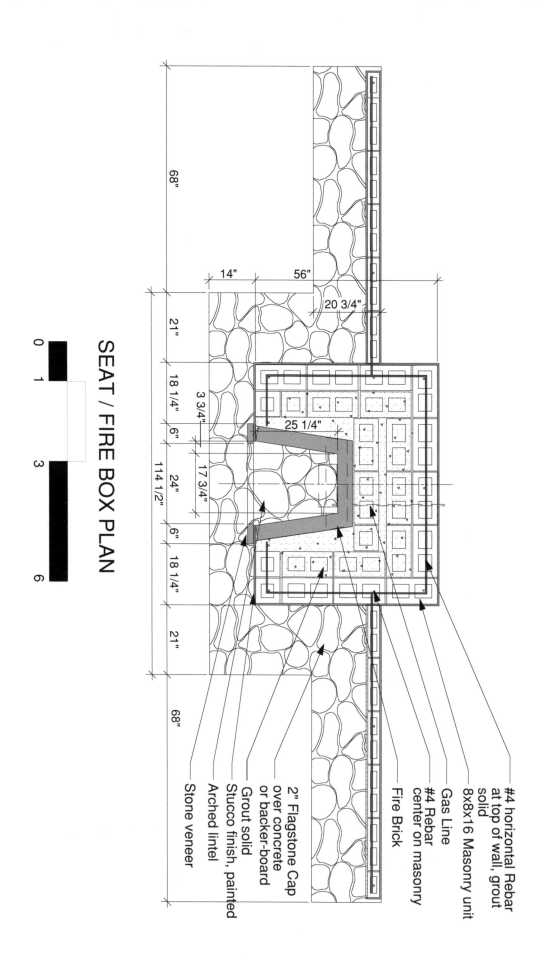

SEAT / FIRE BOX PLAN

68"

14"   56"

20 3/4"

21"   18 1/4"   6"   24"   6"   18 1/4"   21"   68"

3 3/4"   25 1/4"   17 3/4"

114 1/2"

0   1   3   6

#4 horizontal Rebar
at top of wall, grout
solid

8x8x16 Masonry unit

#4 Rebar
center on masonry

Gas Line

Fire Brick

2" Flagstone Cap
over concrete
or backer-board

Grout solid

Stucco finish, painted

Arched lintel

Stone veneer

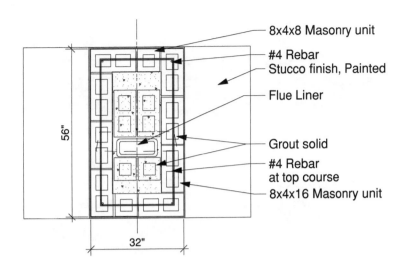

LOWER CHIMNEY PLAN

8x4x8 Masonry unit
#4 Rebar
Stucco finish, Painted
Flue Liner
Grout solid
#4 Rebar
at top course
8x4x16 Masonry unit
56"
32"

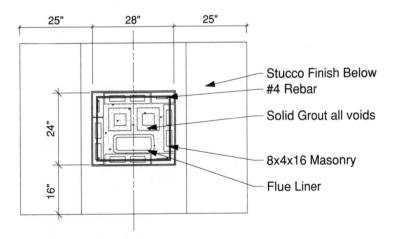

UPPER CHIMNEY PLAN

25"   28"   25"
24"
16"
Stucco Finish Below
#4 Rebar
Solid Grout all voids
8x4x16 Masonry
Flue Liner

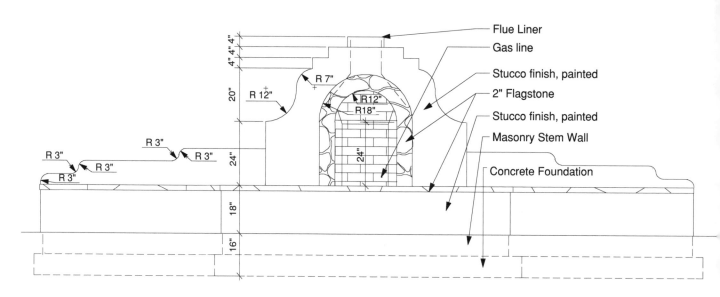

FRONT ELEVATION

0 1 3 6

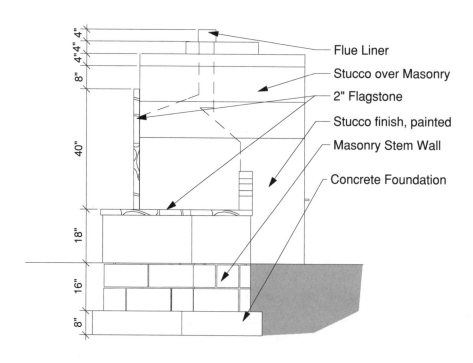

RIGHT SIDE ELEVATION

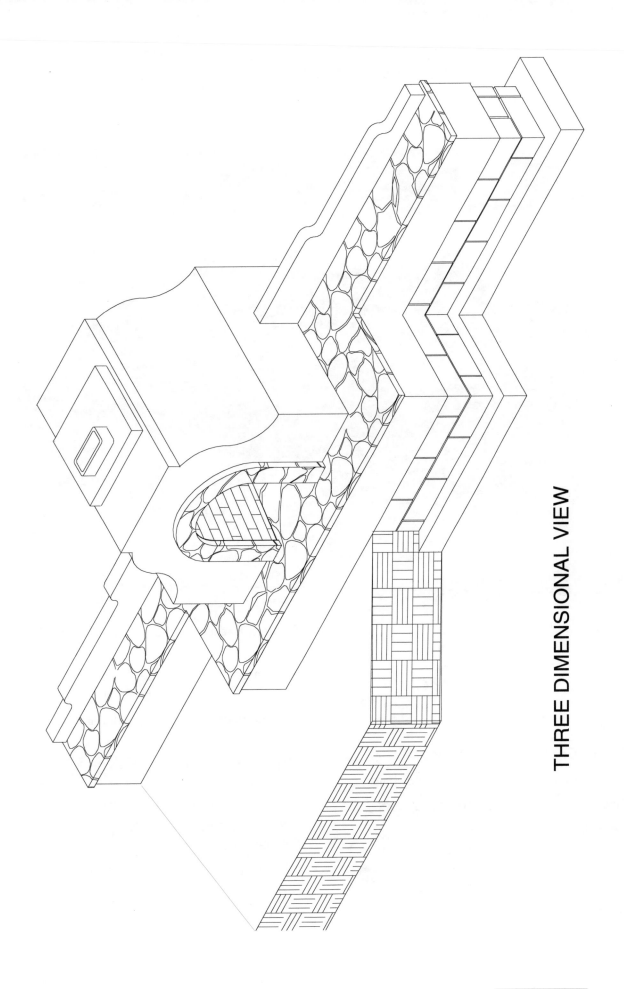

THREE DIMENSIONAL VIEW

Materials List

Concrete Blocks	175 (8×8×16) 50 (8×8×8) 12 (4×8×16) 55 (8×4×16) 12 (8×2×16) solids	**Cement Backer Board**	5 pieces (½"×3'×5')
		Flue Liner	check with local masonry supply for size

Firebricks 75

Premix Concrete 70 (80-pound) bags

Premix Mortar 55 (75-pound) bags

Premix Stucco 3 (90-pound) bags

#4 Rebar 3 pieces (20' long)
3 pieces (40" long)
1 piece (4' long)
25 pieces (32" long)

Rebar Holders 30

Metal Lath 2 pieces (2'×8')

50 square feet of finishing material for hearth and seating

10 square feet of finishing material for raised wall

6 linear feet of finishing material for stone inserted next to fireplace feet corners (see plan)

175 square feet of finishing material for outside surface

Grease Pencil

INSTRUCTIONS

1. According to plan, mark outside edge of foundation

2. Excavate and level the ground for footer

3. Mark the wall for top of footer with grease pencil to indicate where the grade level block is to be placed

4. According to plan, set the rebar holders on the floor of the excavation

5. According to plan, bend and place rebar in rebar holders

6. According to plan, overlap and wire tie necessary rebar

7. Completely fill vertical rebar cells with concrete

8. Mix concrete and pour into footer

9. According to plan, hand lay appropriate courses of block to bring you to firebrick level

10. According to plan, set in template

11. According to plan, repeat instructions on firebrick from design #3 Tuscany

12. Backfill area between fireplace and firebox with appropriate size block or pieces of block

13. Making necessary cuts in block, shape dome of fireplace and concrete

14. According to Beehive #1, install metal lath and stucco

15. According to plan, cut and install cement backer boards with self-tapping screws on sections where stone veneer is attached to fireplace

16. Finish hearth/seats with preselected material (brick, flagstone, tile)

17. Finish raised wall (backer board pieces) with preselected material (brick, flagstone, tile)

CONSTRUCTION PLANS

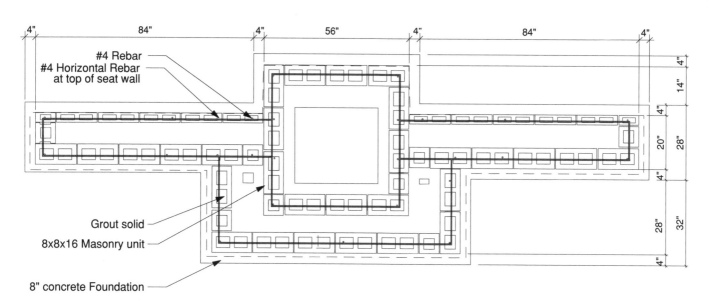

4" | 84" | 4" | 56" | 4" | 84" | 4"

#4 Rebar
#4 Horizontal Rebar at top of seat wall

Grout solid

8x8x16 Masonry unit

8" concrete Foundation

4"
14"
4"
20" / 28"
4"
28" / 32"
4"

FOUNDATION PLAN

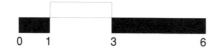

0   1   3   6

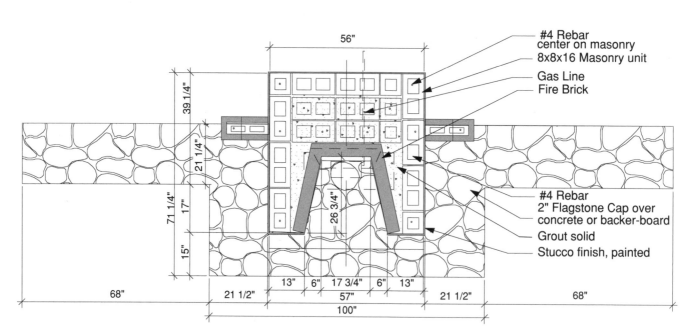

56"

#4 Rebar
center on masonry
8x8x16 Masonry unit
Gas Line
Fire Brick

39 1/4"
21 1/4"
71 1/4"
17"
26 3/4"
15"

#4 Rebar
2" Flagstone Cap over concrete or backer-board
Grout solid
Stucco finish, painted

68" | 21 1/2" | 13" | 6" | 17 3/4" | 6" | 13" | 21 1/2" | 68"
57"
100"

SEAT / FIRE BOX PLAN

0   1   3   6

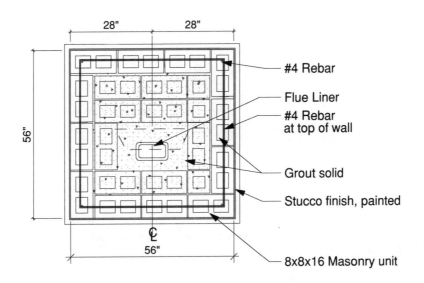

28"   28"

56"

56"

#4 Rebar

Flue Liner

#4 Rebar
at top of wall

Grout solid

Stucco finish, painted

8x8x16 Masonry unit

LOWER CHIMNEY PLAN

0   1   3   6

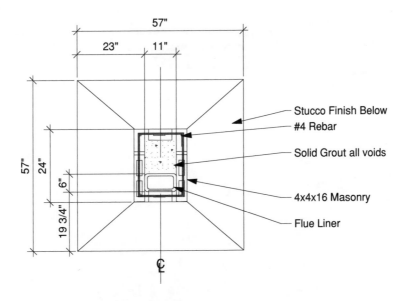

57"

23"   11"

57"

24"

6"

19 3/4"

Stucco Finish Below

#4 Rebar

Solid Grout all voids

4x4x16 Masonry

Flue Liner

UPPER CHIMNEY PLAN

0   1   3   6

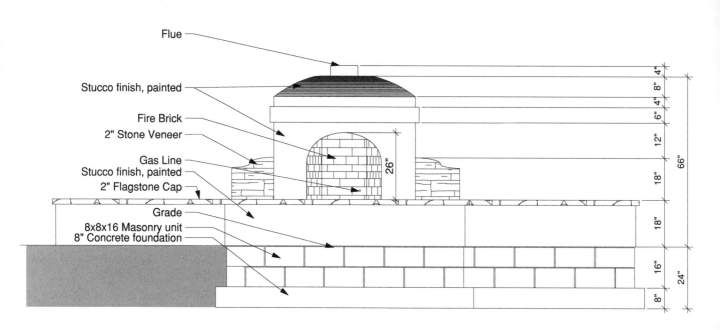

Flue

Stucco finish, painted

Fire Brick
2" Stone Veneer

Gas Line
Stucco finish, painted
2" Flagstone Cap

Grade

8x8x16 Masonry unit
8" Concrete foundation

26"

4"
8"
4"
6"
12"
18"
18"
16"
8"

66"
24"

FRONT ELEVATION

0   1   3   6

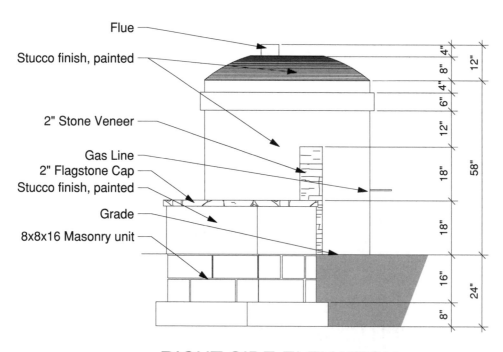

Flue

Stucco finish, painted

2" Stone Veneer

Gas Line
2" Flagstone Cap
Stucco finish, painted

Grade

8x8x16 Masonry unit

4"
8"
4"
6"
12"
18"
18"
16"
8"

12"
58"
24"

RIGHT SIDE ELEVATION

0   1   3   6

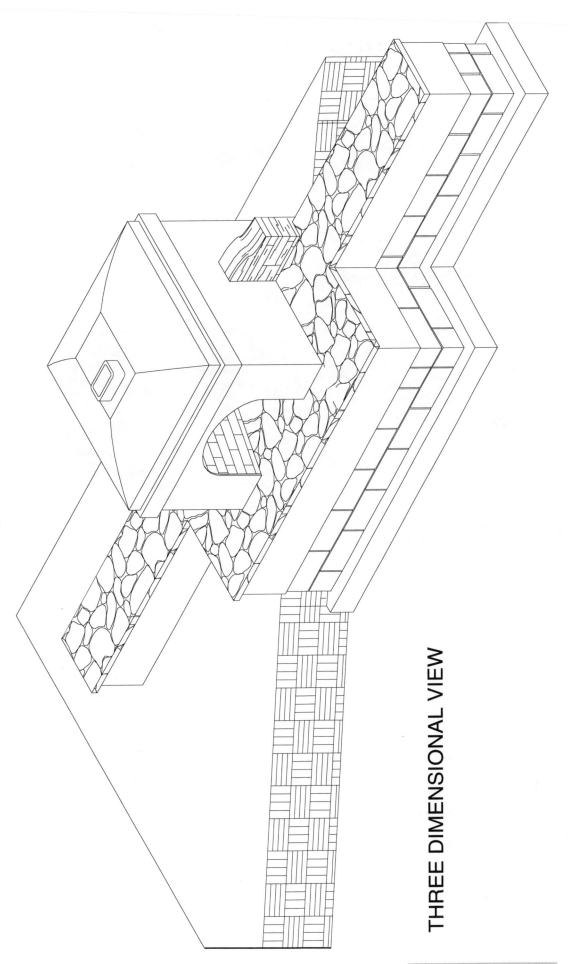

THREE DIMENSIONAL VIEW

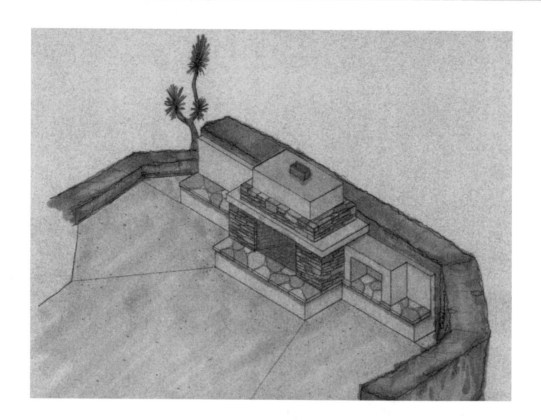

Materials List

Concrete Blocks	240 (8x8x16)		Rebar Holders	50
	35 (8x8x8)		Cement Backer Board	3 pieces (½"x3'x5')
	30 (4x8x16)			
	15 (8x4x16)		Flue Liner	check with local masonry supply for size
	2 (8x4x8)			
	10 (4x4x16)		8" Lintel	(50" long, for fireplace—8" longer than length of door—the size is determined by the builder/owner)
	36 (8x2x16) solids			
	10 (2x4x16)			
Firebricks	75			
Premix Concrete	60 (80-pound) bags		8" Lintel	1 (40" long, for TV niche—8" longer than length of door—the size is determined by the builder/owner)
Premix Mortar	60 (75-pound) bags			
Premix Stucco	3 (90-pound) bags			
#4 Rebar	23 pieces (32" long)		Grout Stop	1 roll (100')
	3 pieces (20' long)			
	4 pieces (8' long)			
	7 pieces (4' long)			
	2 pieces (7' long)			

35 square feet veneer stone

35 square feet of finishing material for hearth/seating

Grease Pencil

INSTRUCTIONS

1. According to plan, mark outside edge of foundation

2. Excavate and level the ground for footer

3. Mark the wall for top of footer with grease pencil to indicate where the grade level block is to be placed

4. According to plan, set the rebar holders on the floor of the excavation

5. According to plan, bend and place rebar in rebar holders

6. According to plan, overlap and wire tie necessary rebar

7. Completely fill vertical rebar cells with concrete

8. Mix concrete and pour into footer

9. According to plan, hand lay appropriate courses of block to bring you to firebrick level

10. According to plan, at this level add additional rebar holders and rebar, tying with wire, if necessary

11. Completely fill vertical rebar cells with concrete

12. According to plan, make necessary cuts in block for fireplace and TV niche area

13. According to plan, set in lintel for fireplace and TV niche

14. Backfill area between fireplace and firebox with appropriate size block or pieces of block

15. According to plan, incorporated into your blockwork, place lintel over fireplace and TV niche openings

16. According to plan, finish firebrick the same as instructed in Tuscany #3

17. According to plan, build chimney frame, inserting rebar and tying together for concrete slab

18. When constructing the chimney, lay grout stop over block cells that are directly over the firebox (see plan)

19. According to plan, install cement backer board

20. Mix and pour concrete on top of form and continue flue and blockwork

21. According to plan, repeat instructions for Beehive #1 and install metal lath and stucco

22. Finish stucco

23. Finish hearth/seats with preselected material (brick, flagstone, tile)

CONSTRUCTION PLANS

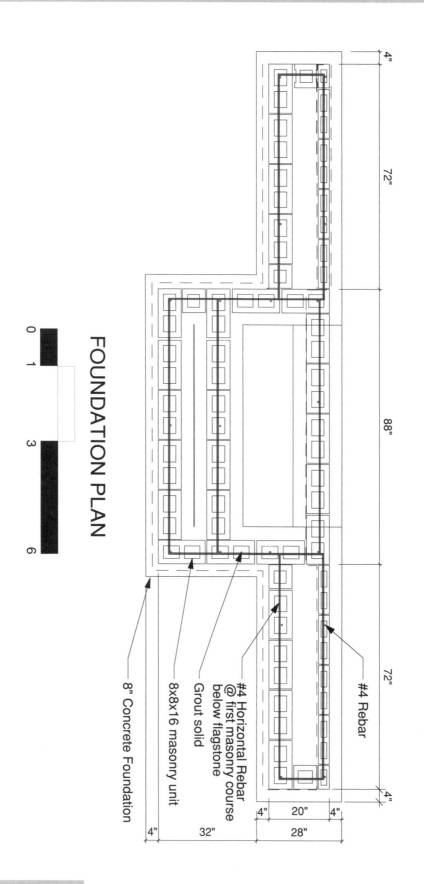

FOUNDATION PLAN

0 1   3   6

8" Concrete Foundation

8x8x16 masonry unit

Grout solid

#4 Horizontal Rebar
@ first masonry course
below flagstone

#4 Rebar

4"   72"   88"   72"   4"

4"   20"   4"
4"   32"   28"

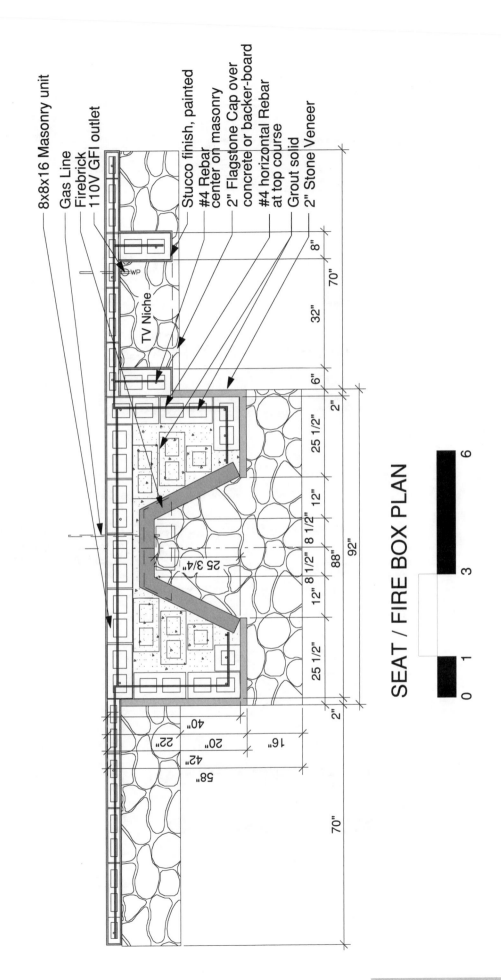

SEAT / FIRE BOX PLAN

8x8x16 Masonry unit
Gas Line
Firebrick
110V GFI outlet
Stucco finish, painted
#4 Rebar center on masonry
2" Flagstone Cap over concrete or backer-board
#4 horizontal Rebar at top course
Grout solid
2" Stone Veneer

TV Niche

WP

8"
70"
32"
6"
2"
25 1/2"
12"
8 1/2"
8 1/2"
12"
25 1/2"
2"
25 3/4"
88"
92"

40"
22"
20"
16"
42"
58"
70"

0 1   3   6

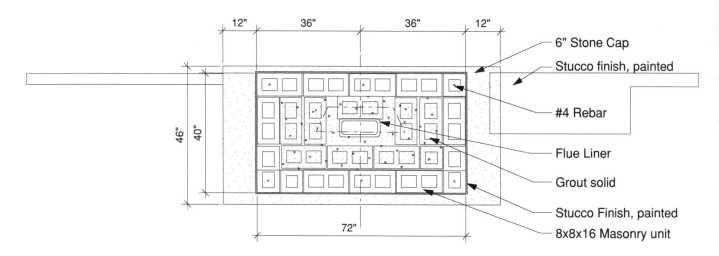

12" 36" 36" 12"

46" 40"

72"

6" Stone Cap

Stucco finish, painted

#4 Rebar

Flue Liner

Grout solid

Stucco Finish, painted

8x8x16 Masonry unit

LOWER CHIMNEY PLAN

0 1 3 6

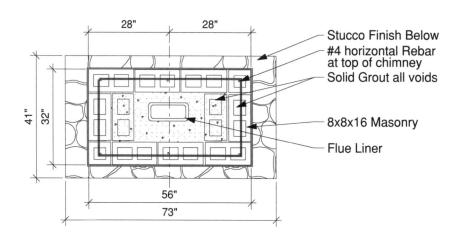

28" 28"

41" 32"

56"

73"

Stucco Finish Below
#4 horizontal Rebar
at top of chimney
Solid Grout all voids

8x8x16 Masonry

Flue Liner

UPPER CHIMNEY PLAN

0 1 3 6

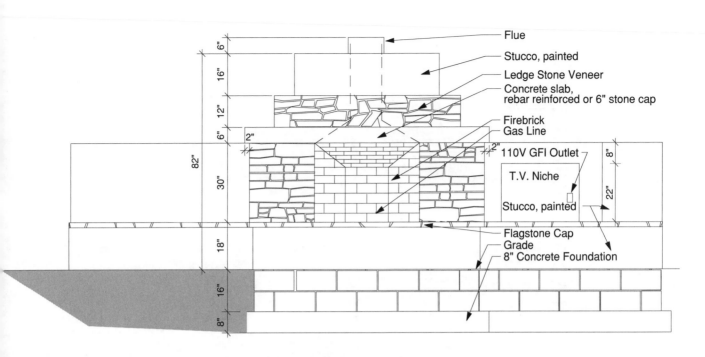

Flue

Stucco, painted

Ledge Stone Veneer

Concrete slab,
rebar reinforced or 6" stone cap

Firebrick
Gas Line

110V GFI Outlet

T.V. Niche

Stucco, painted

Flagstone Cap
Grade
8" Concrete Foundation

6"

16"

12"

6"

2"

2"

82"

30"

8"

22"

18"

16"

8"

FRONT ELEVATION

0 1 3 6

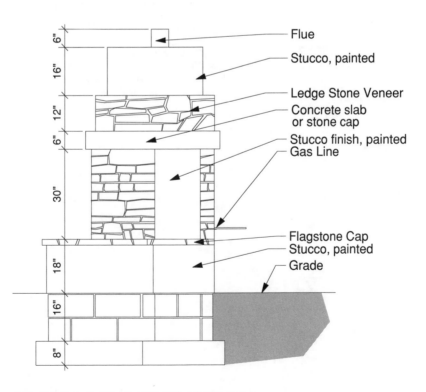

Flue

Stucco, painted

Ledge Stone Veneer

Concrete slab
or stone cap

Stucco finish, painted
Gas Line

Flagstone Cap
Stucco, painted
Grade

6"

16"

12"

6"

30"

18"

16"

8"

RIGHT SIDE ELEVATION

0 1 3 6

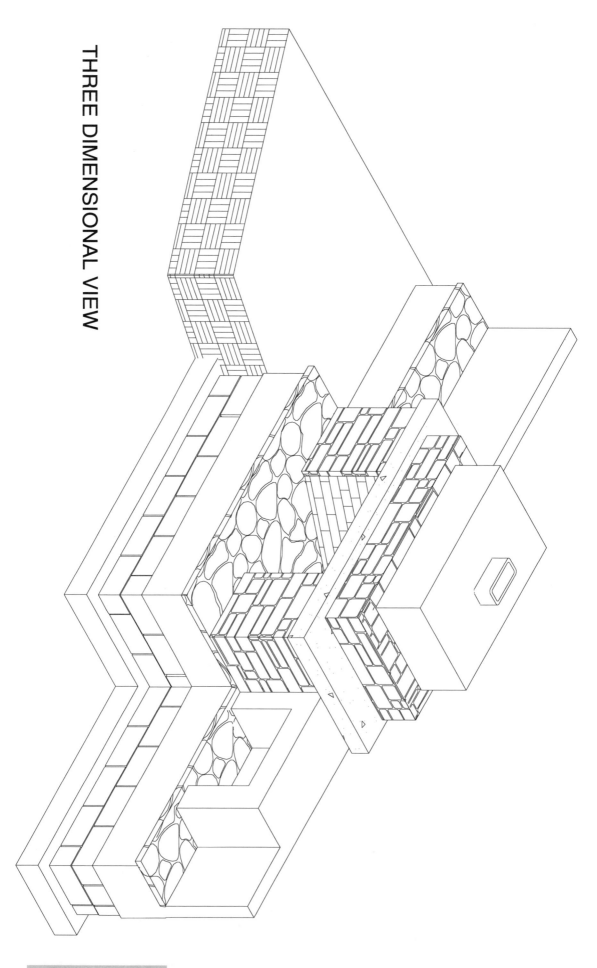

8. Mission with TV

Materials List

Concrete Blocks	270 (8×8×16) 350 (8×8×8) 100 (4×8×8)
Firebrick	300 (4½"×2½"×9")
Premix Concrete	200 (80-pound) bags
Premix Mortar	200 (75-pound) bags or 5 yards sand plus 1 pallet mortar mix
Premix Stucco	1 (90-pound) bag
#4 Rebar	6 pieces (20' long) 5 pieces (6' long) 6 pieces (5' long) 5 pieces (4' long) 15 pieces (3' long)
Rebar Holders	37
Brick Veneer	3000 (3⅝"×2¼"×7⅝" Standard Cored)
Brick Veneer	500 (3⅝"×2¼"×7⅝" Standard Solid)
Brick Ties	500 pieces (1 box)
Metal Lath	2 pieces (1 piece 6"×6" and 1 piece 7'× 20')
Cement Backer Board	2 pieces (½"×3'×5½')
Grout Stop	2 (100') Rolls
Flue Liner	check with local masonry supply for size
8" Lintel	1 (8" wider than doors—the size is determined by the builder/owner)
8" Lintel	1 (8" wider than storage—the size is determined by the builder/owner)
Grease Pencil	

INSTRUCTIONS

1. According to plan, mark foundation

2. Excavate and level the ground for footer and slab

3. Mark the wall for top of footer with grease pencil to indicate where the grade level block is to be placed

4. According to plan, place rebar holder on the floor of the excavation

5. According to plan, bend and place rebar in rebar holders

6. According to plan, overlap and wire tie necessary rebar

7. Completely fill vertical rebar cells with concrete

8. Mix concrete and pour into footer

9. General note: When mortaring in exterior block, at this time you will set in metal brick ties for your brick veneer

10. According to plan, lay courses of block leaving openings for door/storage and beehive opening at the hearth level

11. According to plan, install lintels at designated areas

12. According to plan, hand lay appropriate courses of block to bring you to firebrick level

13. According to plan, set in template

14. According to plan, continue firebrick instructions from design #1 Beehive

15. According to plan, continue block work and sections of rebar, solid filling vertical cells with concrete

16. According to plan, firebrick design should start to change block size at approximately four feet high from firebrick floor (this starts shaping the chimney)

17. According to plan, continue blockwork around firebrick, backfilling between fireplace and firebox with appropriate sizes of block or pieces of block

18. Making necessary cuts in block and firebrick will shape the dome of the fireplace

19. According to plan, install cement backer board

20. According to plan, at approximately eight feet high, rebar will need to be concreted vertically in the block cells providing you with a bond beam (consult local masonry supply store with questions)

21. According to plan, lay in grout stop and continue with firebrick and block, making necessary cuts at appropriate areas of the design

22. According to plan, install flue liner

23. According to plan, start with bottom courses of brick, substituting cored brick in necessary areas (consult local masonry supply store with questions)

24. Clean brick veneer when done (consult local masonry supply store for proper material)

25. Finish the hearth with preselected materials (brick, flagstone, tile, stucco)

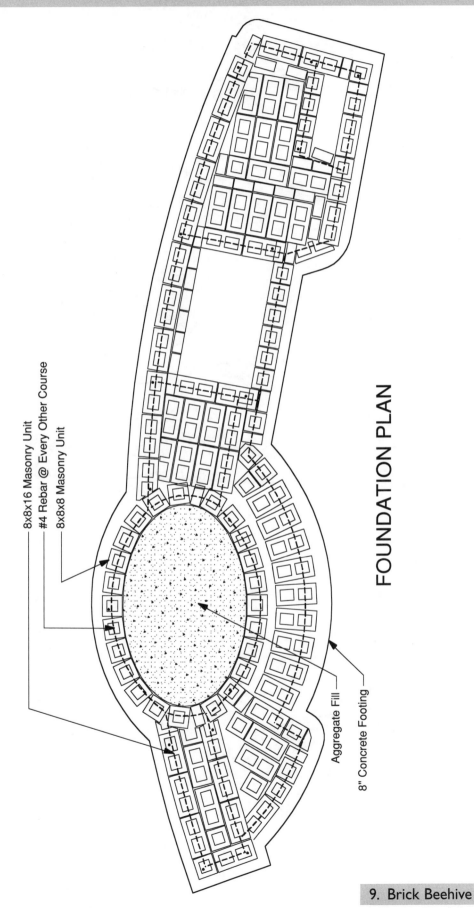

8x8x16 Masonry Unit

#4 Rebar @ Every Other Course

8x8x8 Masonry Unit

Aggregate Fill

8" Concrete Footing

FOUNDATION PLAN

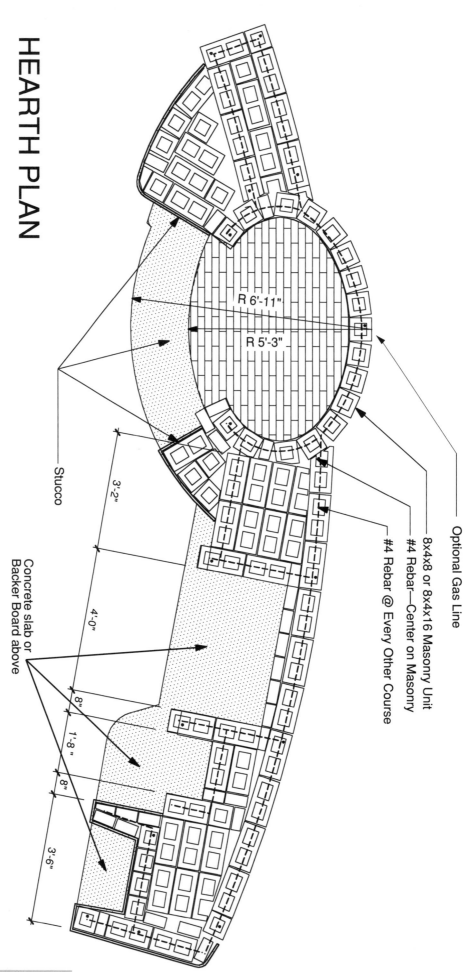

HEARTH PLAN

R 6'-11"

R 5'-3"

Optional Gas Line

8x4x8 or 8x4x16 Masonry Unit

#4 Rebar—Center on Masonry

#4 Rebar @ Every Other Course

Stucco

Concrete slab or
Backer Board above

3'-2"

4'-0"

8"

1'-8"

8"

3'-6"

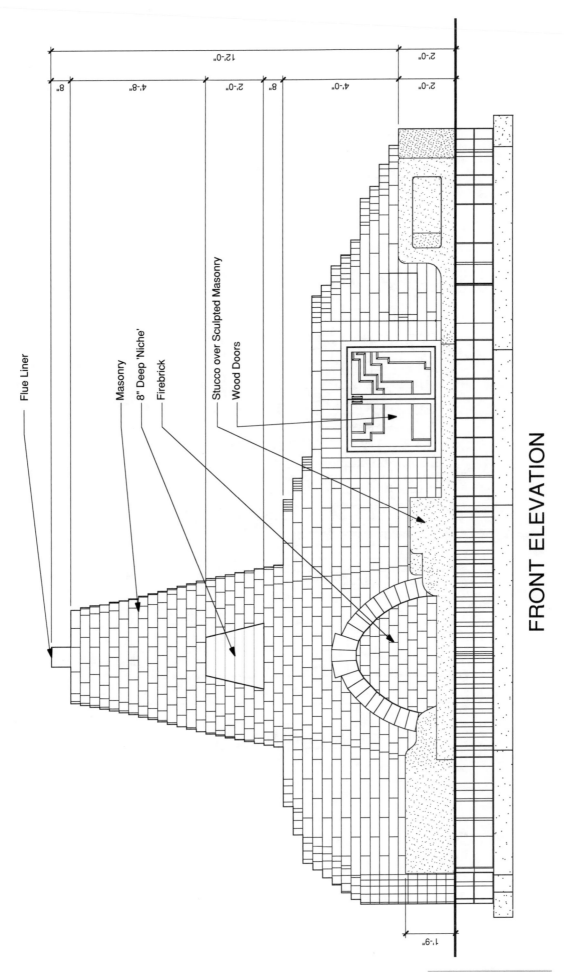

Flue Liner

Masonry

8" Deep 'Niche'

Firebrick

Stucco over Sculpted Masonry

Wood Doors

12'-0"

8"

4'-8"

2'-0"

8"

4'-0"

2'-0"

2'-0"

1'-9"

FRONT ELEVATION

9. Brick Beehive   83

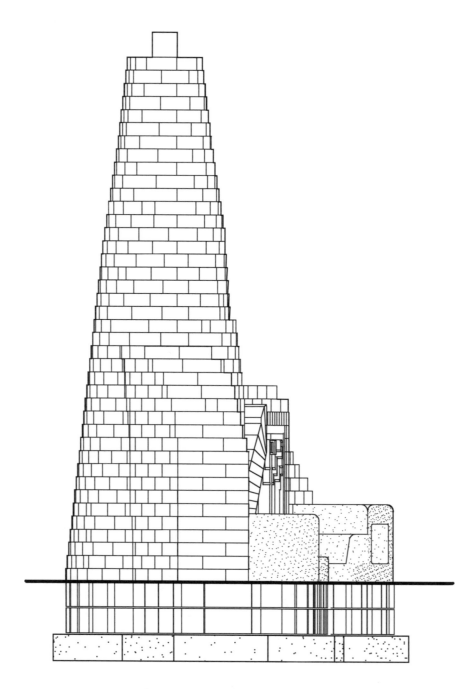

SIDE ELEVATION

9. Brick Beehive

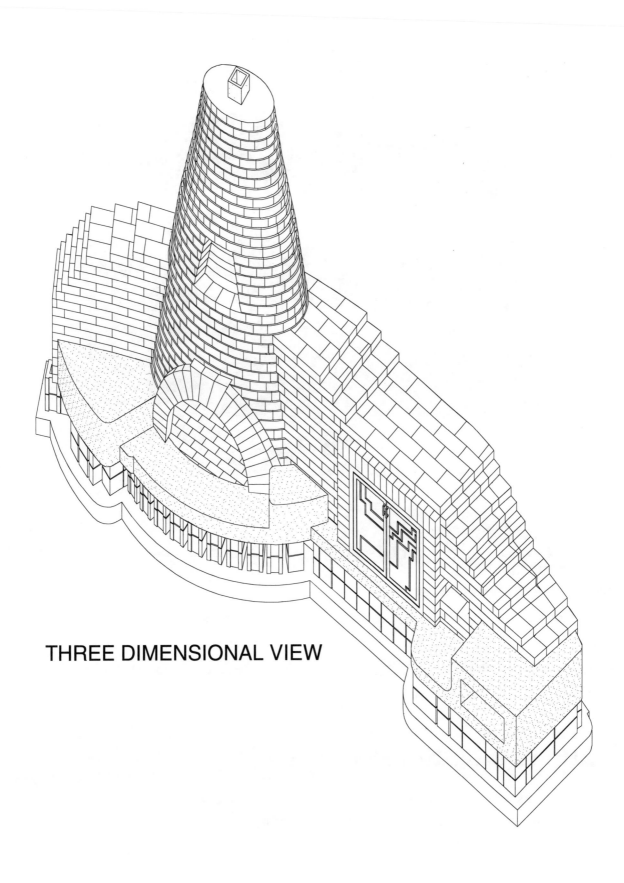

THREE DIMENSIONAL VIEW

Materials List (above ground)

Concrete Blocks	16 (8×8×16)	#4 Rebar	2 pieces (12' long)
Premix Concrete	15 (80-pound) bags	Rebar Holders	12
Premix Mortar	15 (75-pound) bags	12" Round Stake	1
Premix Stucco	1 (90-pound) bag	20 square feet of topping material (brick, stone, tile)	
Firebrick	55 (standard size: 4½"×2½"×9")	Metal Lath	2 pieces (2'×8')

Materials List (in ground)

Concrete Blocks	16 (8×8×16)	Rebar Holders	12
Premix Concrete	15 (80-pound) bags	12" Round Stake	1
Premix Mortar	10 (75-pound) bags	20 square feet of topping material (brick, stone, tile)	
Firebrick	55 (standard size: 4½"×2½"×9")	Mason's Cord	
#4 Rebar	2 pieces (12' long)		

Above Ground Firepit

1. According to Beehive #1, follow instructions for excavation and footer, remembering to run gas line to the center of the diameter (see note below)

2. According to plan, set rebar holders on floor of excavation

3. According to plan, bend and place rebar in rebar holders, overlapping as necessary and tying together with wire

4. According to plan, follow directions on setting blockwork

5. Fill the pit with sand to the top of the foundation

6. Lay firebrick on pit floor, making necessary cuts (firebrick floor can be set either in concrete or laid without concrete)

7. According to plan, continue firebrick to the top, backfill concrete block with pieces of block

8. According to plan, finish top or cap with preselected materials (brick, flagstone, tile)

9. According to Beehive #1 install metal lath and stucco

Note

Gas logs and fire rings should be installed by a licensed contractor. You may also want to purchase (or have made) a cover for your fire pit to keep out the elements. If using propane, it's always good to predetermine where the tanks are to be located (most people want them stored out of sight).

Below Ground Firepit

1. According to plan, mark center point, pound in stake, and mark your diameter using mason's cord

2. According to plan, repeat same procedure above, marking the inside diameter

3. According to plan, excavate and level the bottom of fire pit

4. According to plan, set the rebar holders on the floor of the excavation

5. According to plan, bend and place rebar in rebar holders, overlapping as necessary and tying together with wire

6. Completely fill vertical rebar cells with concrete

7. Mix concrete and pour into footer

8. Install plumbing for gas line into the middle of the pit (see note below)

9. Dry lay firebrick on fire pit floor, marking bricks that need to be cut, and install firebrick up to ground elevation

10. According to plan, continue your blockwork up to ground elevation

11. According to plan, backfill concrete blocks with necessary material and cap off at grade level or slightly above with preselected material (brick, flagstone, tile)

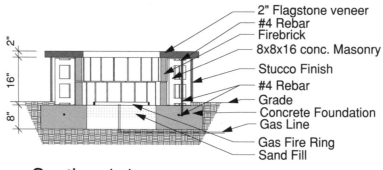

2" Flagstone veneer
#4 Rebar
Firebrick
8x8x16 conc. Masonry
Stucco Finish
#4 Rebar
Grade
Concrete Foundation
Gas Line
Gas Fire Ring
Sand Fill

Section 1-1

ABOVE GRADE

0   1   3   6

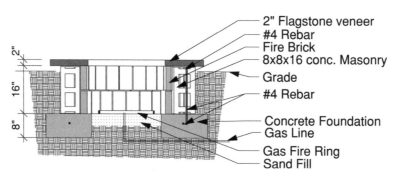

2" Flagstone veneer
#4 Rebar
Fire Brick
8x8x16 conc. Masonry
Grade
#4 Rebar
Concrete Foundation
Gas Line
Gas Fire Ring
Sand Fill

Section 1-1

BELOW GRADE

0   1   3   6

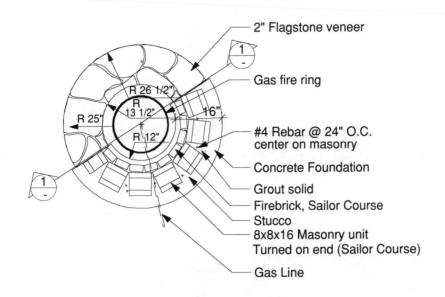

2" Flagstone veneer

Gas fire ring

R 26 1/2"
R 13 1/2"
R 25"
16"
R 12"

1
-

1
-

#4 Rebar @ 24" O.C.
center on masonry

Concrete Foundation

Grout solid

Firebrick, Sailor Course

Stucco

8x8x16 Masonry unit
Turned on end (Sailor Course)

Gas Line

FIRE PIT PLAN

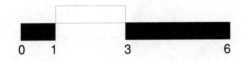

0   1   3   6

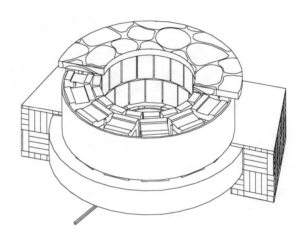

THREE

DIMENSIONAL VIEW

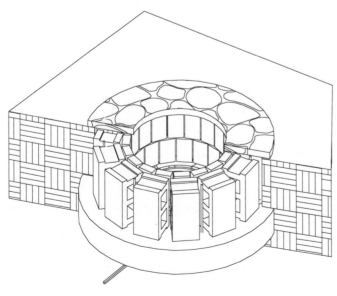

THREE

DIMENSIONAL VIEW

11. Barbecue

Materials List

Concrete Blocks	90 (8x8x16) 21 (8x8x8) 20 (4x8x16) 6 (4x4x16)	**Lintel**	1 (3½"x3½"x¼" steel 8" longer than barbecue door opening—the size is determined by the builder/owner)
Premix Concrete	30 (80-pound) bags		1 (8" longer than opening for door for access to propane tank—the size is determined by the builder/owner)door
Premix Mortar	30 (75-pound) bags		
Premix Stucco	2 (90-pound) bags		
#4 Rebar	1 piece (14' long) 3 pieces (7' long) 1 piece (5' long) 10 pieces (4' long) 12 pieces (32" long)	**Cement Backer Board**	4 pieces (½"x3'x5')
		45 square feet countertop material (brick, flagstone, tile)	
Rebar Holders	12	Barbecue unit and accessories	
		Grease Pencil	

1. According to plan, mark outside edge of foundation

2. Excavate and level the ground for footer

3. According to plan, run sleeve for gas line

4. Mark the wall for top of footer with grease pencil to indicate where the grade level block is to be placed

5. According to plan, set the rebar holders on the floor of the excavation

6. According to plan, bend and place rebar in rebar holders

7. According to plan, overlap and wire tie necessary rebar

8. Completely fill vertical rebar cells with concrete

9. Mix concrete and pour into footer

10. According to plan, hand lay appropriate courses of block to bring you to lintel level, setting lintel in block

General Note
Countertop lighting or side vent lights can be added by modifying the design. This will require you to add electrical conduit and light fixtures to your materials list.

11. According to plan, continue all block-work, making necessary cuts for access doors, air vents and grill area dimensions

12. According to plan, install cement backer board on top of blockwork

13. According to plan, install doors, and air vents

14. According to plan, finish countertop with preselected material (brick, flagstone, tile)

15. According to plan, finish outside block with desired finish (stucco, stone, stone veneer)

16. According to plan, install gas barbecue

CONSTRUCTION PLANS

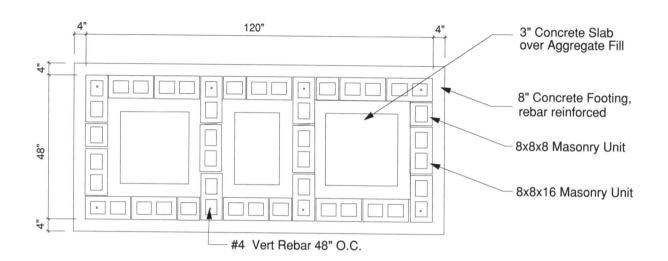

4"   120"   4"

3" Concrete Slab
over Aggregate Fill

8" Concrete Footing,
rebar reinforced

8x8x8 Masonry Unit

8x8x16 Masonry Unit

4"

48"

4"

#4 Vert Rebar 48" O.C.

FOUNDATION PLAN

0   1   3   6

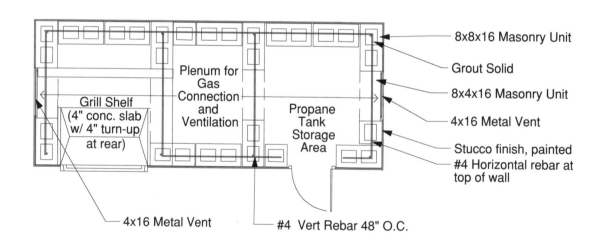

8x8x16 Masonry Unit

Grout Solid

8x4x16 Masonry Unit

4x16 Metal Vent

Stucco finish, painted
#4 Horizontal rebar at
top of wall

Plenum for
Gas
Connection
and
Ventilation

Grill Shelf
(4" conc. slab
w/ 4" turn-up
at rear)

Propane
Tank
Storage
Area

4x16 Metal Vent

#4 Vert Rebar 48" O.C.

GRILL SHELF PLAN

0   1   3   6

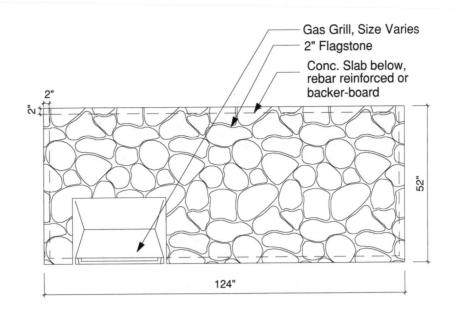

Gas Grill, Size Varies

2" Flagstone

Conc. Slab below,
rebar reinforced or
backer-board

2"

2"

52"

124"

COUNTER TOP PLAN

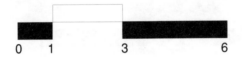

0 1   3   6

Stucco, Painted over
Concrete Masonry Wall

3" Concrete Slab

Ventilated metal door

2" Flagstone

Gas grill

16x24 Vented Metal Door

NOTE: Dimensions
A, C & D dependent
upon grill model

C

A

D

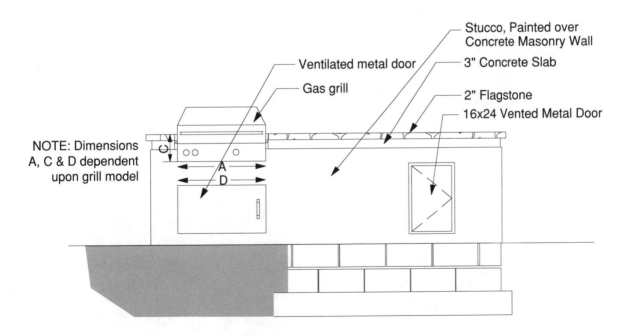

FRONT ELEVATION

0 1   3   6

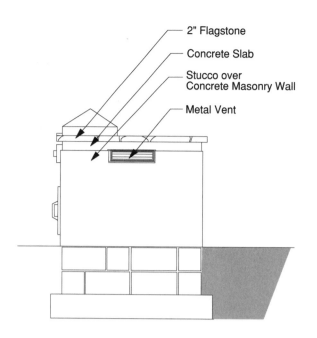

— 2" Flagstone

— Concrete Slab

— Stucco over
Concrete Masonry Wall

— Metal Vent

RIGHT SIDE ELEVATION

0   1   3   6

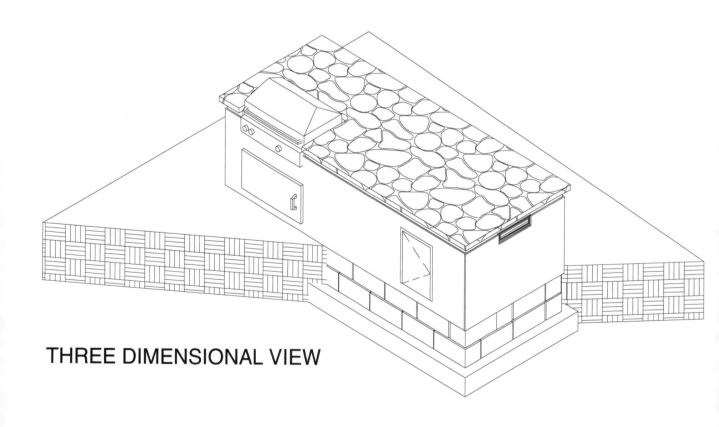

THREE DIMENSIONAL VIEW

12. Barbecue with Serving/Bar Area

Materials List

Concrete Blocks	110 (8×8×16) 15 (8×8×8) 20 (8×4×16) 16 (8×4×16) solids 5 (4×4×16) 5 (4×8×16)	**Lintel**	1 (3½"×3½"×¼" steel 8" longer than barbecue door opening—the size is determined by the builder/owner)
Premix Concrete	30 (80-pound) bags		1 (8" longer than opening for door for access to propane tank—door size up to builder/owner)
Premix Mortar	30 (75-pound) bags		
Premix Stucco	2 (90-pound) bags	**Cement Backer Board**	4 pieces (½"×3'×5')
#4 Rebar	5 pieces (5' long) 2 pieces (14" long) 6 pieces (40" long) 8 pieces (32" long)	50 square feet countertop material (brick, flagstone, tile)	
Rebar Holders	16	90 square feet exterior coating for sides of barbecue and bar (stucco, stone, stone veneer)	
		Barbecue unit and accessories	

Instructions

This design will be built the same way as the previous Barbecue #11 design, except there is additional blockwork (see plan for changes) for the bar serving area.

CONSTRUCTION PLANS

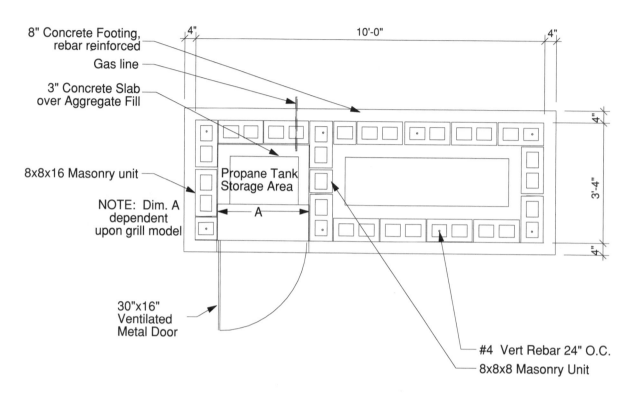

8" Concrete Footing, rebar reinforced

Gas line

3" Concrete Slab over Aggregate Fill

8x8x16 Masonry unit

NOTE: Dim. A dependent upon grill model

30"x16" Ventilated Metal Door

4" 10'-0" 4"

4"

3'-4"

4"

Propane Tank Storage Area

A

#4 Vert Rebar 24" O.C.

8x8x8 Masonry Unit

FOUNDATION PLAN

0   1   3   6

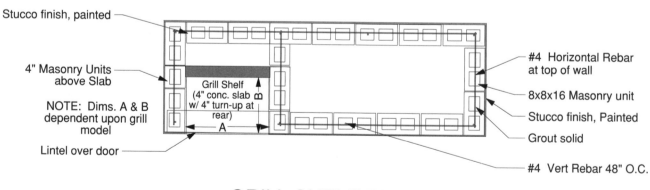

Stucco finish, painted

4" Masonry Units above Slab

NOTE: Dims. A & B dependent upon grill model

Lintel over door

Grill Shelf (4" conc. slab w/ 4" turn-up at rear)

B

A

#4 Horizontal Rebar at top of wall

8x8x16 Masonry unit

Stucco finish, Painted

Grout solid

#4 Vert Rebar 48" O.C.

GRILL SHELF PLAN

0   1   3   6

10'-4"

10'-0"

2" Flagstone

Conc. Slab below,
rebar reinforced
or backer-board

1'-4"
1'-8"

2'-9 3/4"

Conc. Slab below,
rebar reinforced

Gas Grill

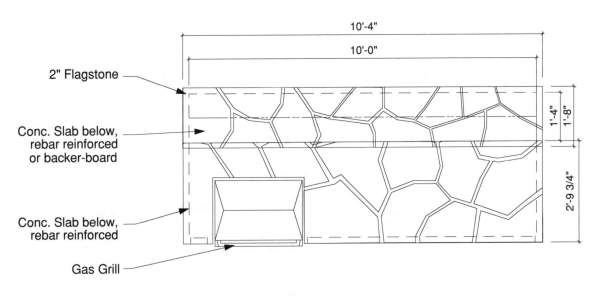

COUNTER PLAN

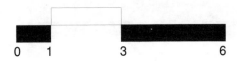

0   1   3   6

Gas Grill

2" Flagstone

NOTE: Dimensions
A, C & D dependent
upon grill model

C

A

D

Vented metal door
size dependent
upon grill model

Stucco painted over
Concrete Masonry
Wall

2"
2"
5"

2"

3'-1"

1'-4"

8"

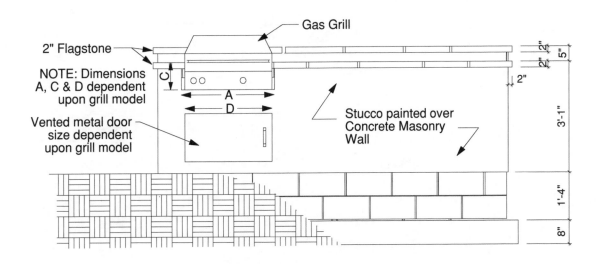

FRONT ELEVATION

0   1   3   6

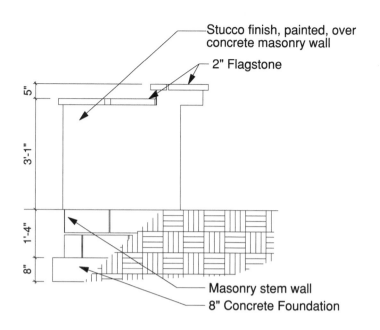

Stucco finish, painted, over concrete masonry wall

2" Flagstone

5"

3'-1"

1'-4"

8"

Masonry stem wall

8" Concrete Foundation

RIGHT SIDE ELEVATION

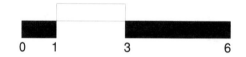

0   1   3   6

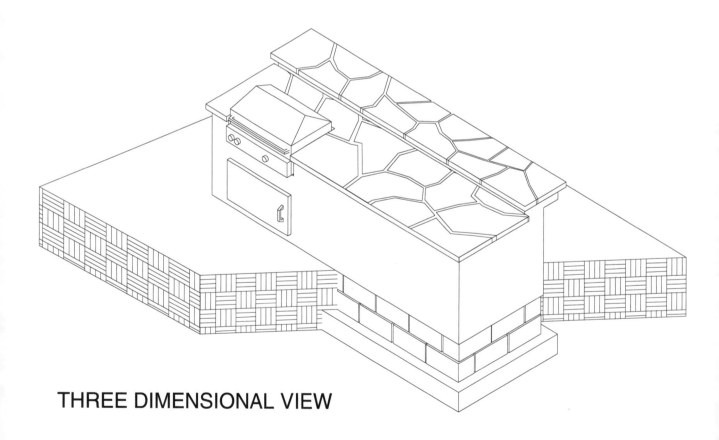

THREE DIMENSIONAL VIEW

Materials List

12" Round Stake	1
Concrete Blocks	10 (8×8×16)
	300 (8×8×8)
	10 (4×8×16)
Premix Concrete	35 (80-pound) bags
Premix Mortar	35 (75-pound) bags
Premix Stucco	2 (90-pound) bags
#4 Rebar	2 pieces (18" long)
	2 pieces (20" long)
	1 piece (2' long)
	6 pieces (4' long)
	1 piece (5' long)
	1 piece (7' long)
	1 piece (8' long)
	1 piece (15' long)
	1 piece (20' long)
	14 pieces (32" long)

Rebar Holders	20
	1 (3½"×3½"×¼" steel 8" longer than barbecue door opening—the size is determined by the builder/owner)
	1 (8" longer than opening for door for access to propane tank—door size up to builder/owner)
Cement Backer Board	8 pieces (½"×3'×5')

80 square feet countertop material (brick, flagstone, tile)

120 square feet exterior coating for sides of barbecue and bar (stucco, stone, stone veneer)

Barbecue unit and accessories

Grease Pencil

INSTRUCTIONS

1. According to plan, mark center point, pound in stake and follow instructions for fire pit #10 above ground

2. According to plan, mark outside edge of foundation

3. Excavate and level the ground for footer

4. According to plan, run sleeve for gas line

5. Mark the wall for top of footer with grease pencil to indicate where the grade level block is to be placed

6. According to plan, set the rebar holders on the floor of the excavation

7. According to plan, bend and place rebar in rebar holders

8. According to plan, overlap and tie necessary rebar

9. Completely fill vertical rebar cells with concrete

10. Mix concrete and pour into footer

11. According to plan, hand lay appropriate courses of block to bring you to lintel level, setting lintel in block

12. According to plan, make necessary cuts in block for access doors, air vents and grill area dimensions

13. According to plan, install rebar which will be set under cement backer board (horizontally)

14. According to plan, at circle area of bar, add additional rebar (horizontally)

15. According to plan, install cement backer board to fit top of barbecue

16. According to plan, install door, and air vents

17. According to plan, finish countertop with preselected material, (brick, flagstone, tile)

18. According to plan, finish outside block with desired finish (stucco, stone veneer, stone)

19. According to plan, install gas barbecue

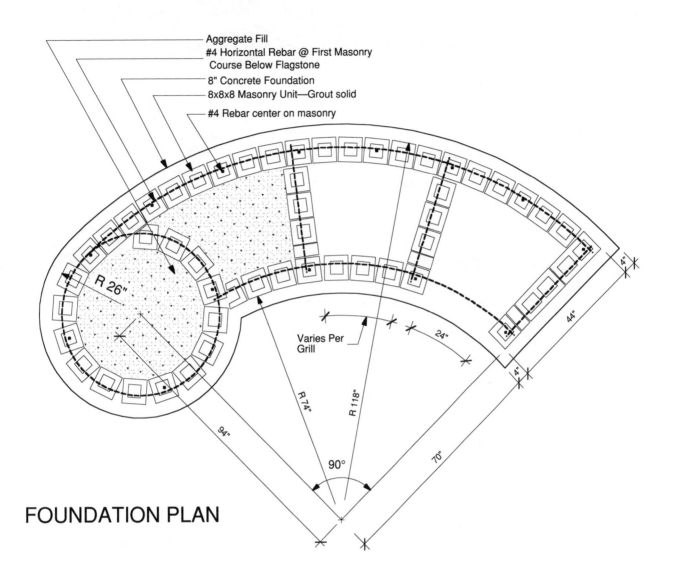

Aggregate Fill
#4 Horizontal Rebar @ First Masonry
 Course Below Flagstone
8" Concrete Foundation
8x8x8 Masonry Unit—Grout solid
#4 Rebar center on masonry

R 26"

Varies Per
Grill

24"

4"

44"

4"

R 74"

R 118"

94"

90°

70"

FOUNDATION PLAN

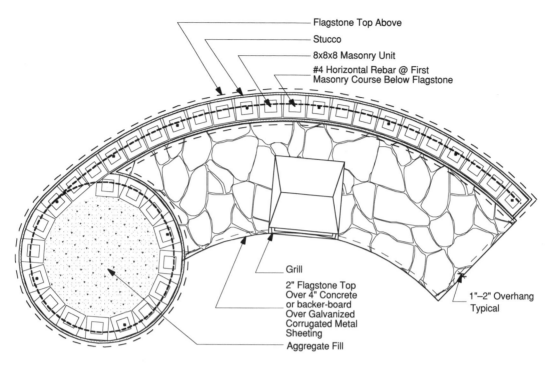

Flagstone Top Above

Stucco

8x8x8 Masonry Unit

#4 Horizontal Rebar @ First
Masonry Course Below Flagstone

Grill

2" Flagstone Top
Over 4" Concrete
or backer-board
Over Galvanized
Corrugated Metal
Sheeting

Aggregate Fill

1"–2" Overhang
Typical

LOWER COUNTER PLAN

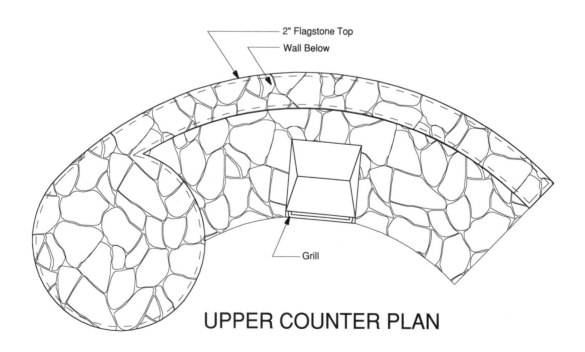

2" Flagstone Top

Wall Below

Grill

UPPER COUNTER PLAN

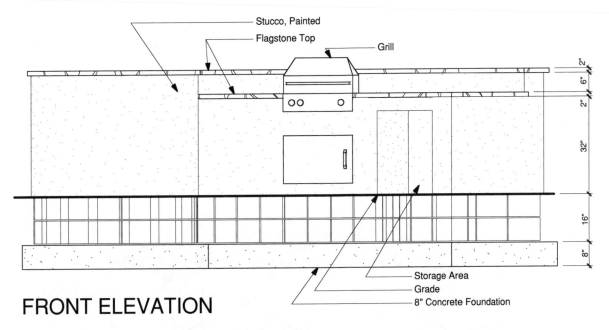

Stucco, Painted
Flagstone Top
Grill

2"
6"
2"
32"
16"
8"

FRONT ELEVATION

Storage Area
Grade
8" Concrete Foundation

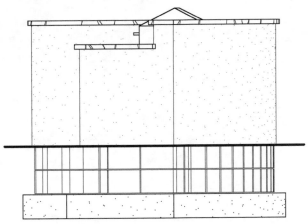

SIDE ELEVATION

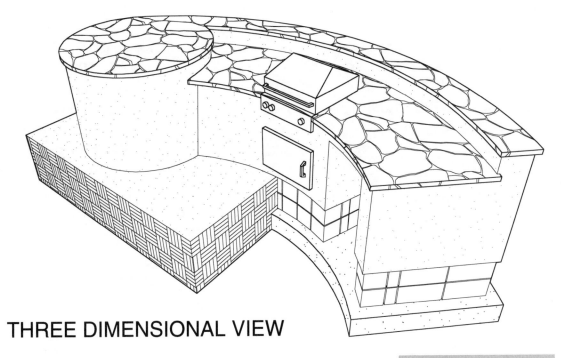

THREE DIMENSIONAL VIEW

14. L-shaped Barbecue

Materials List

Concrete Blocks	130 (8×8×16) 30 (8×8×8) 20 (8×4×16) 5 (8×4×8) 10 (4×8×16)	**Lintel**	1 (3½"×3½"×¼" steel 8" longer than barbecue door opening—the size is determined by the builder/owner)
Premix Concrete	35 (80-pound) bags		1 (8" longer than opening for door for access to propane tank—door size up to builder/owner)
Premix Mortar	35 (75-pound) bags		
Premix Stucco	2 (90-pound) bags	**Cement Backer Board**	5 pieces (½"×3'×5')
#4 Rebar	4 pieces (2' long) 10 pieces (40" long) 5 pieces (5' long) 3 pieces (6' long) 2 pieces (20' long) 20 pieces (32" long)		110 square feet countertop material (brick, flagstone, tile)
			90 square feet exterior coating for sides of barbecue and bar (stucco, stone, stone veneer)
Rebar Holders	20		Barbecue unit and accessories

Instructions

This design will be built the same way as the previous Barbecue #11 design, except the foundation for this structure requires additional materials (listed above) to accommodate the design changes. See plan for changes.

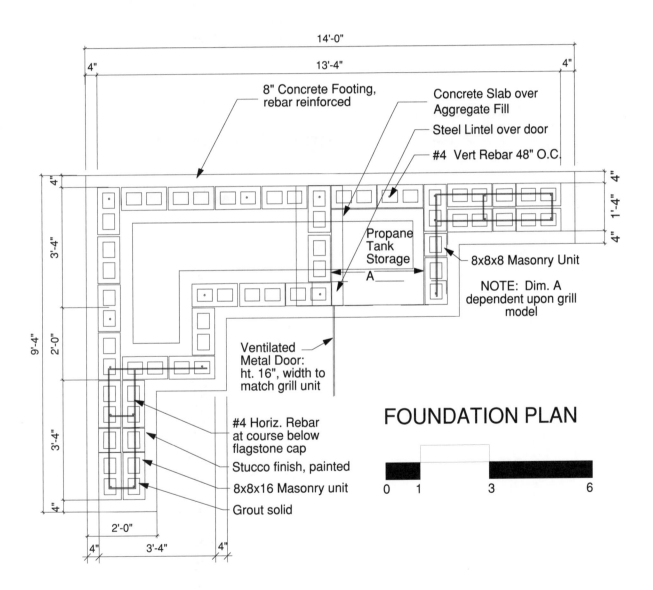

8" Concrete Footing, rebar reinforced

Concrete Slab over Aggregate Fill

Steel Lintel over door

#4 Vert Rebar 48" O.C.

Propane Tank Storage

A____

8x8x8 Masonry Unit

NOTE: Dim. A dependent upon grill model

Ventilated Metal Door: ht. 16", width to match grill unit

#4 Horiz. Rebar at course below flagstone cap

Stucco finish, painted

8x8x16 Masonry unit

Grout solid

FOUNDATION PLAN

0   1   3   6

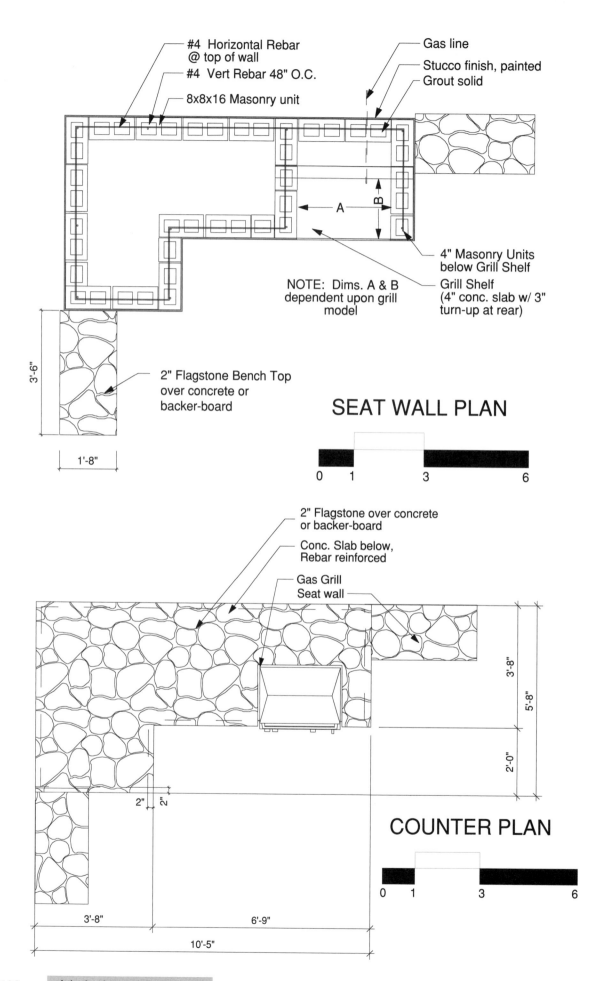

#4 Horizontal Rebar @ top of wall

#4 Vert Rebar 48" O.C.

8x8x16 Masonry unit

Gas line

Stucco finish, painted

Grout solid

A

B

4" Masonry Units below Grill Shelf

Grill Shelf (4" conc. slab w/ 3" turn-up at rear)

NOTE: Dims. A & B dependent upon grill model

3'-6"

2" Flagstone Bench Top over concrete or backer-board

1'-8"

SEAT WALL PLAN

0   1   3   6

2" Flagstone over concrete or backer-board

Conc. Slab below, Rebar reinforced

Gas Grill

Seat wall

3'-8"

5'-8"

2'-0"

2" 2"

COUNTER PLAN

0   1   3   6

3'-8"

6'-9"

10'-5"

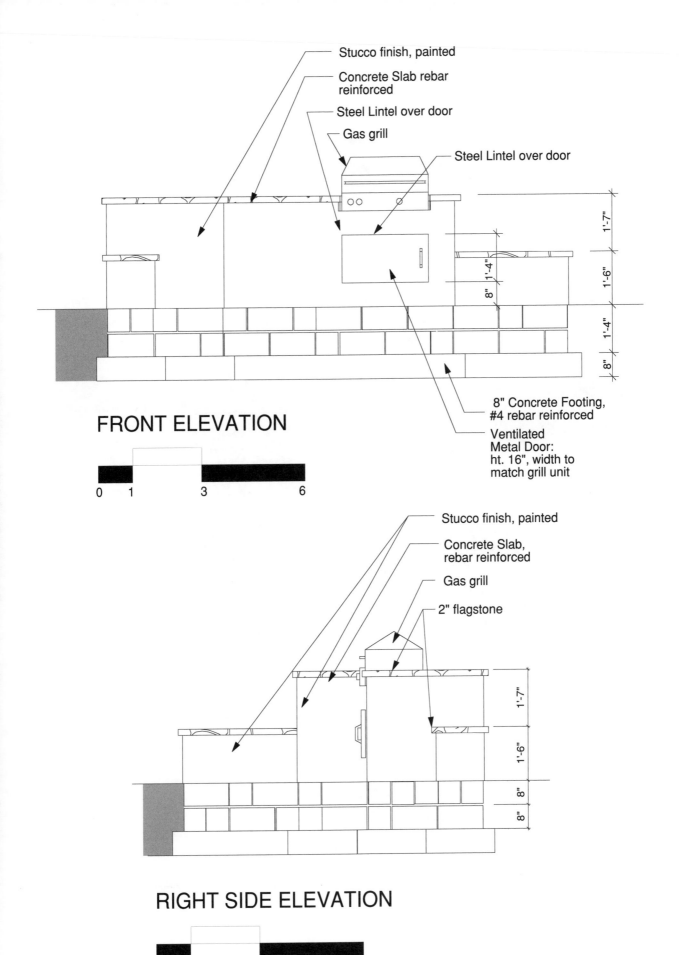

Stucco finish, painted

Concrete Slab rebar reinforced

Steel Lintel over door

Gas grill

Steel Lintel over door

1'-7"

1'-6"

8"   1'-4"

1'-4"

8"

FRONT ELEVATION

8" Concrete Footing, #4 rebar reinforced

Ventilated Metal Door: ht. 16", width to match grill unit

0   1   3   6

Stucco finish, painted

Concrete Slab, rebar reinforced

Gas grill

2" flagstone

1'-7"

1'-6"

8"

8"

RIGHT SIDE ELEVATION

0   1   3   6

THREE DIMENSIONAL VIEW

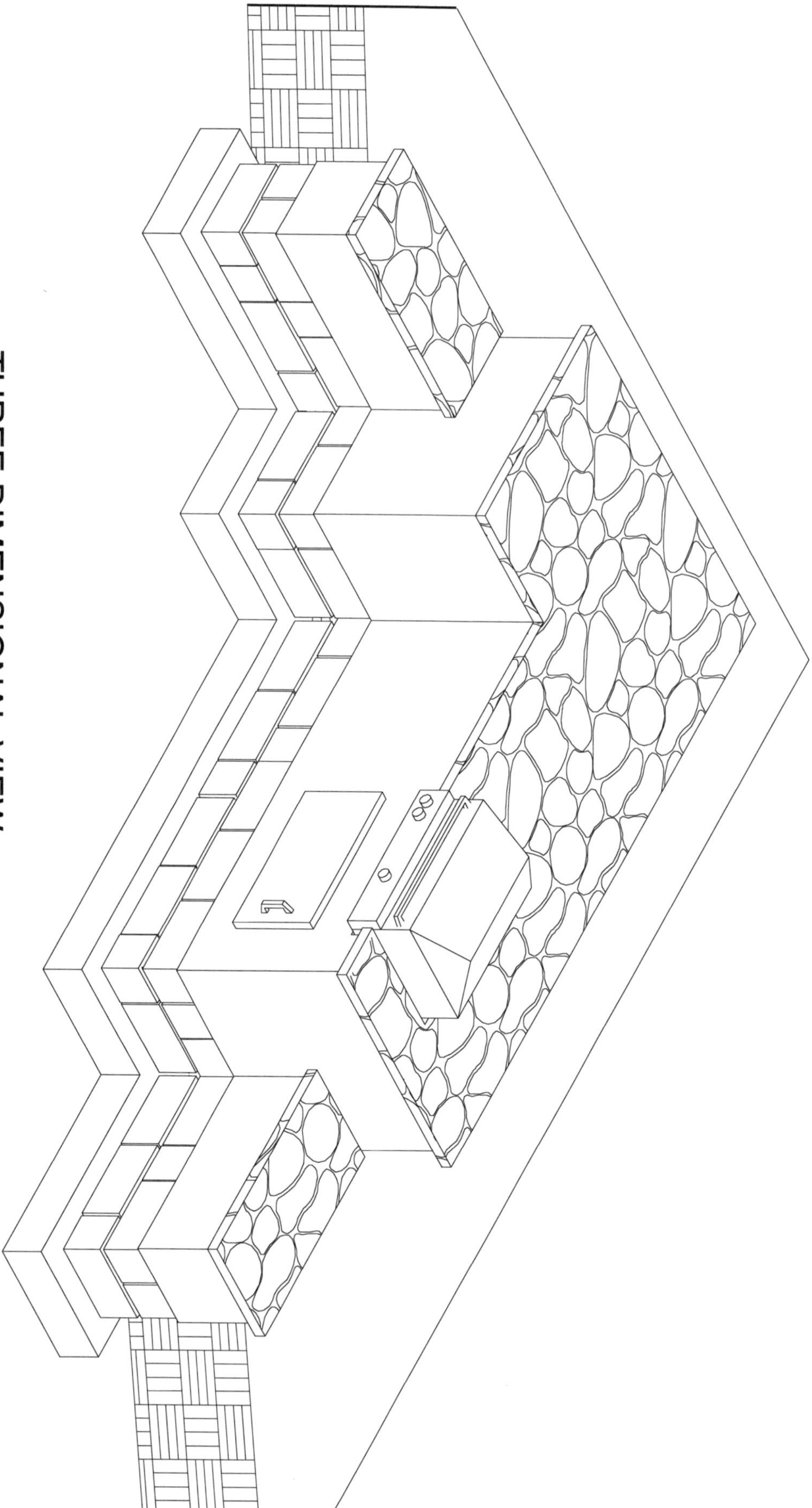

14. L-shaped Barbecue

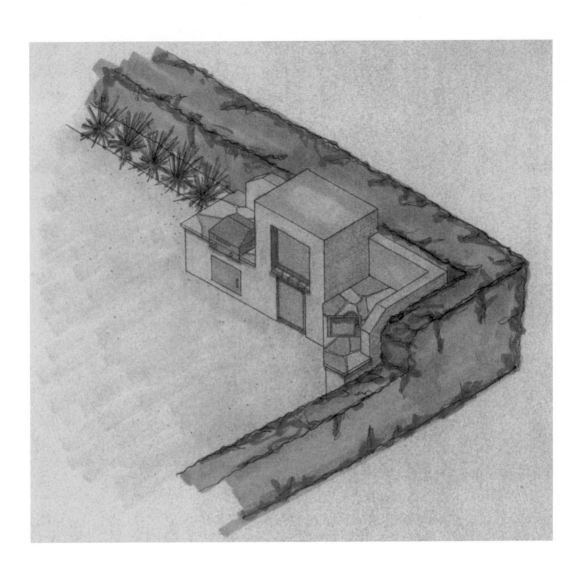

Materials List

Concrete Blocks	300 (8×8×16)	#4 Rebar	10 pieces (3' long)
	45 (8×8×8)		8 pieces (4' long)
	25 (8×2×16)		15 pieces (5' long)
	10 (4×8×16)		2 pieces (6' long)
			6 pieces (8' long)
Premix Concrete	60 (80-pound) bags		4 pieces (10' long)
Premix Mortar	50 (75-pound) bags		3 pieces (20' long)
Premix Stucco	4 (90-pound) bags		11 pieces (32" long)
		Rebar Holders	20

continues ▶

Materials List *(continued)*

10-gauge Concrete Wire	1 piece (5'×8') 2 pieces (5'×3')	**GFCI Duplex Outlets**	2
Cement Backer Board	8 pieces (½"×3'×5')	**Electrical Conduit**	1 (length dependent upon run from main source)
Grout Stop	1 roll (100')	**Cable Line**	1 (length dependent upon run from main source)
Lintel	1 (8" longer than opening for refrigerator—the size is determined by the builder/owner)	**Bar Sink/Faucet**	1 (length dependent upon run from main source)
	1 (8" longer than opening for TV—the size is determined by the builder/owner)	**Copper Tubing for Bar Sink**	1 (length dependent upon run from main source)

60 square feet countertop material (brick, flagstone, tile)

270 square feet exterior coating for sides of barbecue and bar (stucco, stone, stone veneer)

Barbecue unit and accessories

Grease Pencil

Lintel *(continued)*

1 (8" longer than opening for door for access to propane tank—door size up to builder/owner)

1 (8" longer than opening for sink access door—the size is determined by the builder/owner)

1. According to plan, mark outside edge of foundation

2. Excavate and level the ground for footer

3. According to plan, run sleeves for gas line, electrical conduit, and water line for bar sink

4. Mark the wall for top of footer with grease pencil to indicate where the grade level block is to be placed

5. According to plan, set the rebar holders on the floor of the excavation

6. According to plan, bend and place rebar in rebar holders

7. According to plan, overlap and wire tie necessary rebar

8. Completely fill vertical rebar cells with concrete

9. Mix concrete and pour into footer

10. According to plan, hand lay appropriate courses of block to bring you to lintel level, setting lintel in block

11. According to plan, continue all blockwork making necessary cuts for access doors, air vents, television, bar sink, grill, and refrigerator

12. According to plan, place a roll of grout stop at the top of the block level for television and refrigerator

13. According to plan, lay in rebar horizontally across top course of block to support countertop, barbecue, television and sink

14. According to plan, install cement backer board on top of barbecue

15. According to plan, continue laying rebar horizontally and block for television area and raised wall area

16. According to plan, cement backer board on top of all blockwork

17. According to plan, install doors, air vents, GFCI's, and bar sink

18. According to plan, finish countertop with preselected material (brick, flagstone, tile)

19. According to plan, finish outside block with desired finish (stucco, stone veneer, stone)

20. According to plan, install gas barbecue, television, bar sink, and refrigerator

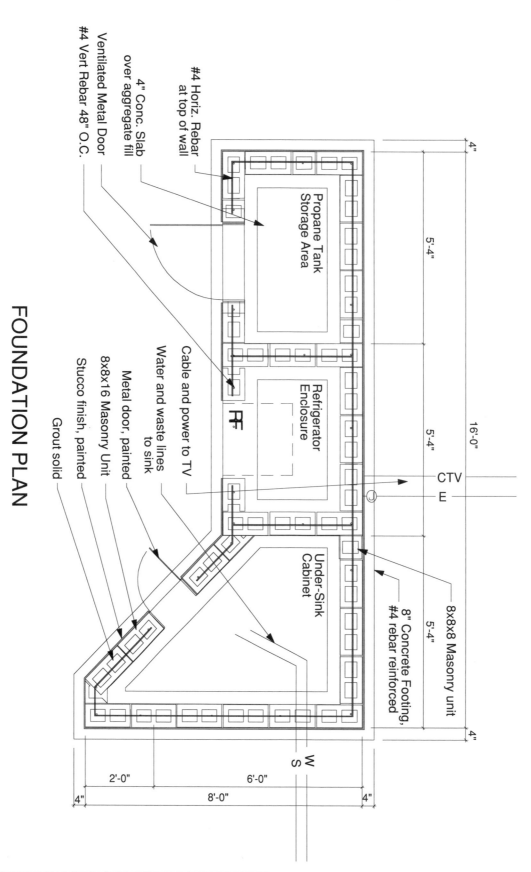

FOUNDATION PLAN

#4 Horiz. Rebar at top of wall

4" Conc. Slab over aggregate fill

Ventilated Metal Door

#4 Vert Rebar 48" O.C.

Cable and power to TV

Water and waste lines to sink

Metal door, painted

8x8x16 Masonry Unit

Stucco finish, painted

Grout solid

Propane Tank Storage Area

Refrigerator Enclosure

Under-Sink Cabinet

8x8x8 Masonry unit

8" Concrete Footing, #4 rebar reinforced

RF

CTV

E

4"

5'-4"

16'-0"

5'-4"

5'-4"

4"

2'-0"

6'-0"

8'-0"

4"

4"

W

S

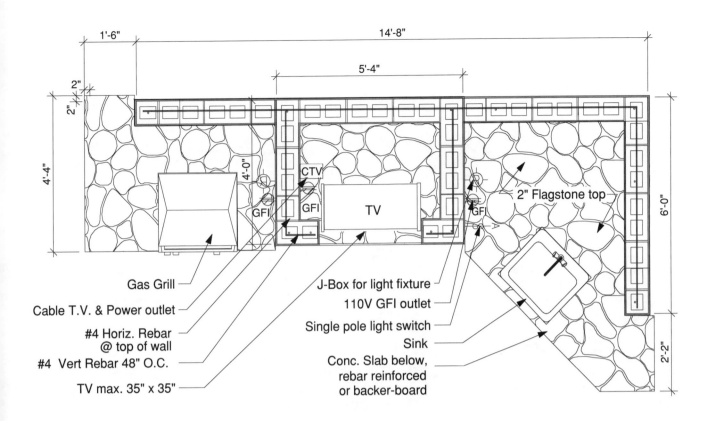

1'-6"   14'-8"

5'-4"

2"

2"

4'-4"

4'-0"

6'-0"

2'-2"

CTV

GFI GFI TV GFI

2" Flagstone top

Gas Grill

Cable T.V. & Power outlet

#4 Horiz. Rebar @ top of wall

#4 Vert Rebar 48" O.C.

TV max. 35" x 35"

J-Box for light fixture

110V GFI outlet

Single pole light switch

Sink

Conc. Slab below, rebar reinforced or backer-board

COUNTER PLAN

0   1   3   6

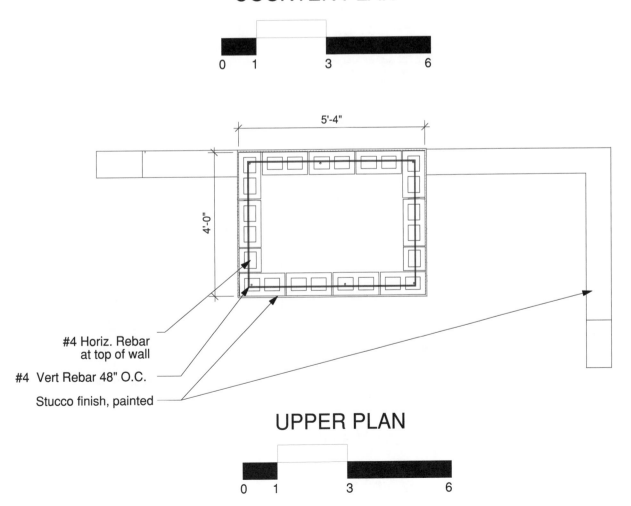

5'-4"

4'-0"

#4 Horiz. Rebar at top of wall

#4 Vert Rebar 48" O.C.

Stucco finish, painted

UPPER PLAN

0   1   3   6

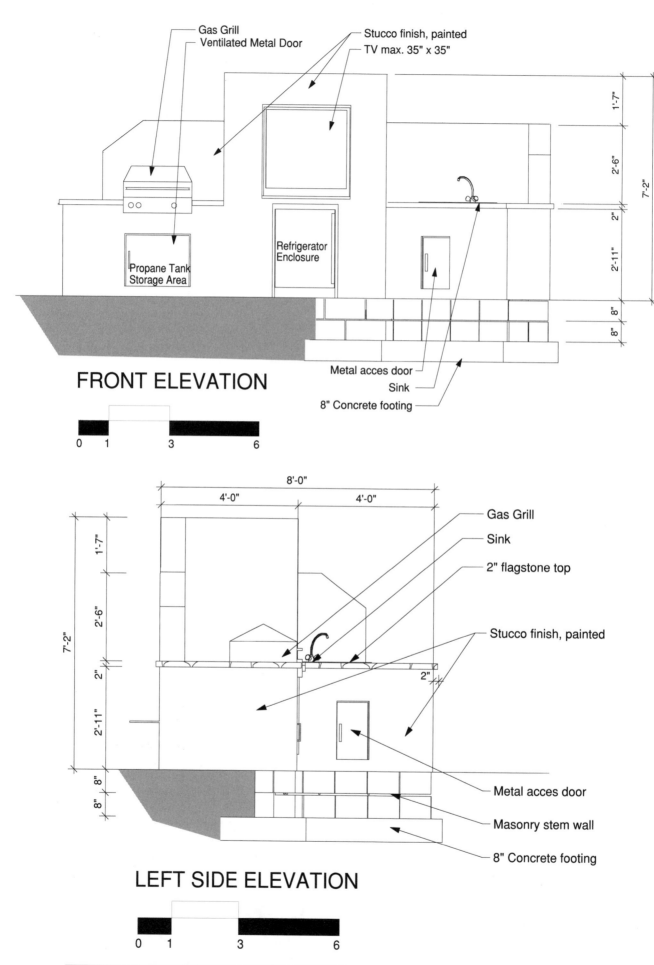

Gas Grill
Ventilated Metal Door

Stucco finish, painted
TV max. 35" x 35"

1'-7"

2'-6"

7'-2"

2"

Propane Tank
Storage Area

Refrigerator
Enclosure

2'-11"

8"

8"

FRONT ELEVATION

Metal acces door
Sink
8" Concrete footing

0 1   3   6

8'-0"

4'-0"   4'-0"

Gas Grill

Sink

2" flagstone top

1'-7"

2'-6"

7'-2"

Stucco finish, painted

2"

2'-11"

2"

8"

8"

Metal acces door

Masonry stem wall

8" Concrete footing

LEFT SIDE ELEVATION

0 1   3   6

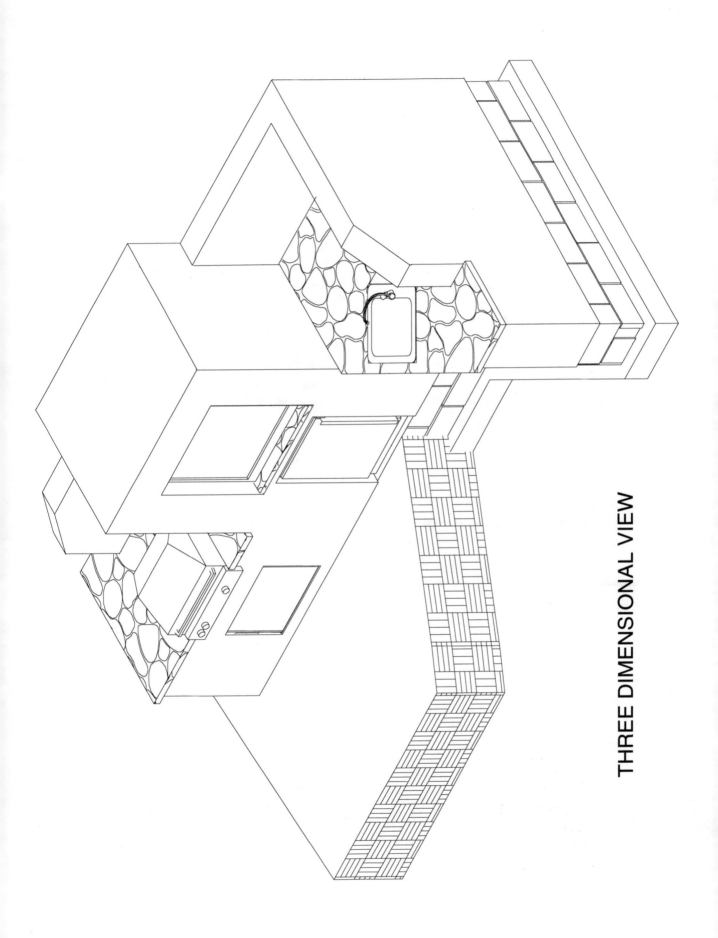

THREE DIMENSIONAL VIEW

Resource List

Arizona Gas Products
Arthur Cikins
16050 N. 76th Street, Suite 104
Scottsdale, AZ 85260
Phone: (480) 609-8855
e-mail: azgasproducts@uswest.net
website: ArizonaGasProducts.com

College of Architecture and Environmental Design
Arizona State University
Tempe, AZ

Creative Environments/Design & Landscape
Tom Baird
2128 E. Cedar Street
Tempe, AZ 85281
(480) 777-9305
e-mail: TomB@CreativeEnvironments.com
Created design plans #3, 4, 5, 6, 7, 8, 13,14, and 15 in this book. Created the designs in the photos on pages A-2, A-3, A-7 (bottom), A-9 (bottom0, A-11, A-14 (top), A-15 (top)

DK Interior Concepts
Owner: Diana Karam
94 S. Main Street
Yardley, PA 19067
Phone: (215) 493-4319
Fax: (215) 493-7219
e-mail: Dkconcepts@aol.com

Gordon Benham Studios
Principal: Gordon Benham
Designer: Brian Thompson
(602) 565-9191
e-mail: Crashoverider1@msn.com
Created the designs in the photos on pages 1, A-4 (top), A-15 (bottom)

Kirshner Landscapes
Howard Kirshner
473 Durham Road (Route 413)
Newtown, PA 18940
(215) 968-7730
website: www.KirshnerNurseries.com
Kathy James for Kirshner Landscapes, created the Designs in the photos on pages A-5, A-10

Mail Boxes, Etc.
8912 E. Pinnacle Peak Road, F-8
Scottsdale, AZ 85255
Phone: (480) 585-8066
Fax: (480) 585-4303

Marvel Brick Source
Mark de Mayo
16602 N. 32nd Street
Phoenix, AZ 85032
Cell: (602) 971-8912
Store: (602) 971-2710

Salcito Custom Homes, Ltd.
8714 E. Vista Bonita Drive, Suite 101
Scottsdale, AZ 85255
(480) 585-5065

Shiloh Custom Homes
15955 N. Dial Boulevard, Suite 1
Scottsdale, AZ 85260
Phone: (480) 951-0585
Fax: (480) 348-9722
Built the fireplace (design #9) that is shown on the front cover

Sonoran Oasis Images, Inc.
Kathy James
(267) 880-1474
Created the designs in the photos on the front
cover, the bottom photo on the back cover, and on
pages A-1, A-4 (left), A-5, A-6, A-7, A-8, A-10, A-12, A-13, A-14
(above and right), and A-16

Urban Design Associates, Ltd. (UDA)
Principal Architect: Lee Hutchinson
8150 N. 8th Place
Scottsdale, AZ 85258
(480) 905-1212

74-894 Lennon Place, Suite C-1
Palm Desert, CA 92260
(760) 773-9733

Witte Architecture
Principal Architect: Joe Witte
Associates: Chuck Hill, Karen Ouzt, Russ Saunders
2910 E. Windrose Drive
Phoenix, AZ 85037
Phone: (602) 765-6236
Fax: (602) 765-6237
e-mail: WitteArch@fastq.com

Portraits by Reg

Herb Stokes
5450 Lakeshore Drive
Tempe, AZ 85283
(480) 839-3709

Photography Credits

Mark Boisclair Photography, Inc.
Mark Boisclair
2512 E. Thomas Road, Suite 1
Phoenix, AZ 85015
(602) 957-6997
e-mail: MarkBPhoto@aol.com

Landscape Illustrations

Darrel Biggs
Darrel@yahoo.com

Index